THE LEGEND OF BELLE STARR

Stoney Hardcastle

Good Luck

Stoney Hardcastle

LIFE AND LEGEND OF BELLE STARR
Certain assumptions and interpretations of historical facts were made by the author.

Indian Nations Publishing Company
701 West Blair, Wilburton, Oklahoma 74578

Reprint by INDIAN NATIONS PUBLISHING COMPANY, 701 WEST BLAIR, WILBURTON, OK 74578

Mail orders: Write the above, send check or money, include $1 for postage and handling.

OTHER PUBLICATIONS AVAILABLE BY AUTHOR

OKIE DICTIONARY $1 plus .50 postage

ROBBERS CAVE STATE PARK, History and Legend $3 plus .50 postage

CREATIVE WRITING, SKILLS and TECHNIQUES
Text On Learning Professional Writing
Published by Eastern Oklahoma State College $10 plus $1.50 postage

Indian Nations Publishing Co.
701 W Blair
Wilburton, Ok 74578

ISBN 0-9653874-0-2

THE LEGEND OF
BELLE STARR

Dedicated to my wife, Sue,
and my editors,
Pat and Harold Starbuck

CHAPTER ONE

"It's a girl, John." The frontier doctor smiled.

In 1846 John and Eliza Shirley pulled up stakes in their native Virginia and settled in Jasper County, Missouri. There they bought a large tract of land and started a thoroughbred horse farm.

Good horses were in high demand along the western frontier and the operation was an immediate success. Soon the Shirleys became prosperous. They were active in social affairs, and respected community leaders. But there was a void in their otherwise enjoyable life. They loved their two young sons, Preston and Ed, but they longed for a daughter.

Then on February 5, 1848, their prayers and wishes were fullfilled—a baby girl arrived, a beautiful child with jet-black eyes. Even before her prayers were answered, Eliza had the fashionable name Myra Belle ready for christening her new daughter.

Myra Belle enjoyed her early years on the farm. She played, attended a country school and was the constant companion of her older brothers. By the time she could walk they taught her to ride and shoot a gun. She became an expert at both.

Eliza Shirley was not happy seeing her daughter grow into a tomboy. But she was consoled by her husband, John. He reasoned there was plenty of time for Myra Belle to receive proper training to become a fashionable young lady.

John Shirley was a shrewd businessman. When Myra Belle was eight he entered a new business venture. Accepting a good offer for his horse farm he moved his family to Carthage, Missouri. There he established a hotel, livery stable and blacksmith shop. He chose his location well, at a crossroads with forks to California, Independence, Fort Smith, the Indian Territory, and Texas. The Shirley stop soon became known all along the frontier.

Shirley had other things in mind when he moved his family to Carthage. He was well educated and wanted his children to have the same opportunity.

The new business prospered and soon the Shirleys became one of the most respected families around Carthage. Myra Belle was enrolled in the exclusive Carthage Female Academy. The Shirleys wanted their daughter to have all the op-portunities.

Myra Bell rewarded her parents, even beyond their fondest dreams. She excelled in school and became a top student. In addition to the basic cur-riculum she studied piano and drama, and was con-sidered to have extraordinary talents in both. Yet her main interests were horses and guns. Every spare minute she could afford away from her studies she spent with her brothers riding and shooting.

Adding more prestige to the family, John was ap-pointed judge. This gave Myra Belle a new interest. She became her father's self-appointed law clerk, spending many hours studying law. For relaxation she spent the long evenings in the hotel lobby listening to travelers' tales. She liked best the ones about wild-shooting outlaws and Indians.

Then suddenly the Shirleys' good life ended. What John Shirley prayed wouldn't happen, did—the Civil War. Violence, pillage, rape, murder soon swept over the border states. Missouri was divided. Some favored the North, some the South, but most couldn't make up their minds. Citizens joined first one side then the other trying to survive. Many were at the mercy of the numerous marauding guerrilla bands which swarmed the borders.

The Kansas Jayhawkers struck terror in the hearts of the Missourians as they raided across the border. The notorious, ruthless rebel leader William C. Quantrill organized a band of guerrillas to strike back at the Jayhawkers. He assembled a small army of some of the country's fiercest fighters in one group. Cole Younger, his brothers, the James boys and Jim Dancer were just a few of the raiders who went on to write infamous history.

The Shirleys were steadfast Southern sympathizers. Myra Belle idolized Quantrill and his raiders. She hated "Damned Yankees" and Jayhawkers. Secretly she talked her brother Ed into organizing his own guerrilla band. With admiration and excitement she questioned Ed after each raid. "How many bluebellies did you get?" She pleaded with Ed to let her ride with him. His reply was always, "No, you are only fifteen and a lady."

The war became more violent and bitter. In 1863, Union troops occupied Missouri, but were harrassed day and night by the hard-riding guerrilla bands. Quantrill's bloody raid on Lawrence,

Kansas, in August, 1863, brought great satisfaction to the Southerners, but quick retaliation by the Union forces. They attacked and burned much of Carthage, headquarters of many of the guerrilla bands. During the action Ed Shirley was killed.

At the funeral Myra Belle sat dry-eyed, seemingly in a trance. She stared straight ahead, eyes hard and face set in an emotionless mask. She left the services before the rest of her family.

John and Eliza Shirley noticed their daughter's strange behavior during the funeral service. They didn't understand her lack of emotion, because they knew of her deep love for her brother. Worried, they rushed home after the services. Their worries were confirmed. When they arrived home Myra Belle was waiting astride their big, black prize stallion, Sambo. She was rigged for traveling, a bedroll and other gear tied behind the saddle. But what alarmed the Shirleys most were the two big pistols strapped around their daughter's waist. The guns—Starr double-action Army forty-fours—had belonged to her dead brother.

"Myra Belle, what are you up to?" John Shirley demanded.

She looked her father straight in the eye. John Shirley couldn't believe the voice was his daughter's. "Father, I'm going to get those damned Yankees. They killed Ed. They are going to pay, damn them."

Shirley jumped from the buggy and grabbed Sambo's reins. "You're not going, Myra Belle. You're only a child."

But the revenge-crazed girl was determined. She jerked the reins hard and stuck her heels to Sambo. The big horse reared and spun, throwing John Shirley to the ground.

Myra Belle threw a kiss over her shoulder. "Goodbye, Father and Mother. Goodbye."

CHAPTER TWO

Myra Belle let Sambo have his head. He hadn't been ridden in several days and wanted to romp. She didn't rein him in until the smoking ruins of Carthage were out of sight. She rode off the main road into a clump of trees, took stock and laid her plans. The late afternoon sun showed about three hours of daylight. It would be a hard all-night ride to reach her destination—the Cherokee Nation, Indian Territory. There was no time to lose. She kicked the big horse into a long ground-eating gait.

Before her brother Ed was killed, he had told her about a big guerilla hideout just across the Missouri line in the Cherokee Nation. He had detailed the camp's location and she was sure she would have little trouble finding it.

Sambo's easy gait ate up the miles. Myra Belle pulled her dead brother's hat low over her eyes to shield off the hot sun. As darkness approached she spotted a farmhouse a short distance off the road. She decided to stop and see if the farmer would sell her some feed for Sambo and maybe something for herself. She carried a canteen of water and some food, but wanted to save them for later. Before riding up to the house she dismounted and hid her guns in some weeds, not wanting to arouse suspicion. Most of the rural people were friendly to guer-

11

rillas, but some were Yankee sympathizers. She didn't want to take chances.

The farmer and his family were friendly and fed Myra Belle and her horse. During the meal she learned a big troop of Union Cavalry had ridden by earlier in the day. No doubt these were some of the same troops who had burned Carthage and killed her brother.

After questioning the family in detail about the troops, Myra Belle mounted Sambo and rode into the night. There was a quarter moon. By midnight she picked up the Feds' trail. They were sticking to the main road and heading straight for the Indian Territory. Then her mind jumped. They were going to attack the guerrilla camp in the Cherokee Nation! She had to get around the troops and warn the guerrillas.

She pulled Sambo to a stop. It was dark. She didn't know the country. The Feds were on the main road. To get around them would mean circling through the brush. It would be impossible. Then she saw a light about a mile ahead. It was a fire. The Feds had made camp for the night. That would make it easier to slip past them.

Dismounting, Myra Belle studied the stars for direction, then tried to make her eyes penetrate the dark dense brush which lined the road. It was going to be rough, finding her way through the darkness. Then she threw back her head and chuckled aloud. "Why all the worry? I'll ride right through that Fed camp."

Sure it would work. She would be a trader's daughter on her way home to the Cherokee Nation. Many travelers had said she looked like a Cherokee with her black eyes and hair. Her name would be

Chouteau. The famous trading family name was widely known. She had met Colonel Chouteau several times when he stopped at the Shirley Hotel, and had spent many enjoyable evenings listening to his stories.

With her plan thought out Myra Belle rode toward the Union Camp. She was expecting the challenge when it came. "Halt! Who goes there?"

"Sir, sir, I'm Mary Chouteau." She used her drama training, raising her voice to an excited pitch.

The sound of a female voice in the dark wilderness stunned the guard. Myra Belle walked Sambo closer. By the dim moonlight she made out the outline of a guard with a rifle. Sambo's nose was almost touching the sentry. The guard shouted, "Halt right there, or I'll shoot you."

"Sir, don't shoot."

Another voice off in the darkness shouted. "What's up?"

"A woman on a horse, I think. Bring a torch."

The other sentry approached with a pine-pitch torch blazing. Myra Belle knew her act must be good. She swung from the saddle and stepped in front of Sambo facing the guard with the torch. Pinching her face in fright she asked, "Sir, are you Union Soldiers?"

The sentries were shocked to find a beautiful young girl alone in the darkness, dressed as a man with two big guns strapped to her waist. The men just stood a few seconds and gaped. Myra Belle was relieved when the one with the torch spoke. "Little miss, what in the world are you doing out here in the night by yourself?"

"On my way home over in the Indian Territory."

"That's a long ways," the other guard cut in. "Better take her to the major and let him talk to her."

The one with the torch said, "I guess that would be best." He turned to Myra Belle. "Leave your horse here and come with me."

She didn't like the idea of leaving Sambo, but it was no time to argue. Still acting she handed the reins to the other guard. "Sir, Sambo is gentle, but watch him. Sometimes he doesn't like strangers." The last part was true. She patted the big horse's nose and followed the guard with the torch.

As Myra Belle and the guard walked she studied his face by the torch light. He was young, blond, round-faced, and his accent told her he was from the North. If they were alone, he would die. She fought back her emotions.

They walked by the light of torches stuck on trees. The summer night air was hot and humid. The camp was asleep. Myra Belle could see soldiers scattered about stretched on blankets. Snores from the men and the popping of night creatures were the only sounds. They broke from the trees into a small clearing. In the center was a squat tent with a fire in front. Near the small fire a man sat cross-legged studying a piece of paper that looked like a map.

The man heard the approaching footsteps and glanced up. He stared hard. Then he jumped to his feet wiping at his sweaty brow. "What do we have here?"

"This lady rode into camp, Major."

The major moved closer, eyeing Myra Belle. His gaze stopped on the guns. "Ma'am, move over here under the light. I want a better look at you."

Myra Belle moved closer. The major's eyes moved

from her head down to her feet then back to the guns.

"I'll be darned, you are just a child. What on earth are you doing running around out here in the darkness with those guns? Danged if they won't weigh more than you will."

Myra Belle forced a weak smile. "I'm on my way home, sir."

"Where?"

"Cherokee Nation, sir."

"Your name?"

"Chouteau, Mary Chouteau."

"Miss Chouteau, what are you doing up here in Missouri?"

"My folks sent me all the way to Carthage for some medicine. My mother is very sick." She could tell by the officer's face, her act was working. "When I got to Carthage"—she paused and took a deep breath—"the Union troops had burned it." Again she fought back her emotions and said, "Good enough for those Rebs."

The major grinned. "So you are with the Union?"

"Yessir, my father says the Rebs must be brought to tow."

"Your father is a wise man. Only way to get those bushwhacking Rebs is to smoke them out."

There was another urge to kill, Myra Belle held her composure. "That is exactly what Father says."

The major shifted his feet. "Well, young lady, I think we better put you up for the night. This is bushwhacker country. It isn't safe for a man, let alone a young lady."

She was expecting the reply and had an answer ready. "Oh no, sir. Thanks but I can't. My mother is very sick and needs me. And they will have heard of the battle at Carthage and be worried sick about me. I must get home. I can take care of myself."

"I believe you," the major said. His attention was still on Myra Belle's guns. "May I ask where you got those revolvers? Starr double-action, latest thing out. May I see one?"

There was nothing else to do. She took one of the guns from its holster and handed it to the major butt-first. She had to think fast. Her answers must be convincing. Her brother Ed had told her he had taken the guns from the body of a Union officer. What if they were marked and the major recognized them? "They belong to my father. He bought them in St. Louis, I think."

The major caressed the revolver, raising and lowering the hammer, balancing it in his hand, then leveling it. "Fine weapon, I've heard they may issue us some of these soon."

After several minutes of toying with the gun he handed it back to Myra Belle. "Too bad you're not a Reb, I would take those guns as booty." The major grinned, then turned to the guard. "Take the little lady back to her horse and escort her through the camp."

"Thank you, sir," Myra Belle replied.

As she and the guard walked back to the sentry post, Myra Belle asked some innocent-sounding questions. "How many men in this troop? And where are you going?"

The guard, eager to make conversation with the pretty young miss, readily supplied the answers. "We are about two-hundred strong. We don't know our orders, but it is rumored we are supposed to turn east tomorrow into Arkansas, make camp and rest a bit. I sure hope that is true."

When they reached the sentry post the guard

politely helped her mount, and walked alongside as they moved through the camp. When they reached the edge of the camp the young soldier asked, "Miss Chouteau, would you give me your address? I would like to write to you."

For the first time Myra Belle used her devilish female charms on a man. She bent and kissed the young soldier on the cheek. "I would love that. Write to Mary Chouteau, Fort Gibson, Cherokee Nation." To kiss her enemy aroused a strange excitement. She hoped she had given him a kiss of death.

Before the astonished guard could reply, she stuck her heels to Sambo and raced into the night. About two miles from the camp she rode off the road into some dense woods. By the light of the quarter moon she found a small opening in the thick brush. Dismounting she unsaddled the big stallion and unpacked her gear. With a lead rope she staked Sambo in a thick patch of dewy grass. She didn't think he would leave her, but she wasn't taking chances.

With Sambo taken care of she unrolled her bedroll. Camping out wasn't a new experience—she had been on many outings with her brothers. She stretched out on her blanket using her saddle for a pillow. Staring up at the stars her thoughts were many and scattered—the war, her dead brother, her mother, father. The Feds were going to camp over the line in Arkansas. She believed the rumor the soldier had told her. A sweet excitement swept her mind. She would follow and scout the Union troops and get the exact location of their camp. She would ride to the guerrilla camp in the Indian Territory and give them the information. The resting Union troops would be careless and unsuspecting. They could be wiped out. It would work. She would have revenge.

Excitement gave way to exhaustion. The revenge-maddened girl slept.

Myra Belle jumped awake. It was the rattling of the Union Cavalry passing on the nearby road. They were moving early, before sunup. She ran to Sambo, petting him for fear he would whinny. She was sure the soldiers couldn't see her through the dense brush. Just in case they might, she saddled up, rolled her gear and made ready to ride. She had no doubt that the calvary horses couldn't catch her big thoroughbred. The thought of a race excited her, but now was not the time.

After the troops passed Myra Belle decided to scout the countryside before trailing them. She rode from the woods into a small meadow. Then a rooster crowing off to her right caught her attention. The rooster meant a house and possibly a hot meal was nearby. She rode toward the sound which was coming from beyond a wooded draw. After a short distance she picked up a wagon road which wound across the draw into a new-ground clearing.

Myra Belle pulled up Sambo. On the far side of the field was a cabin, barn, and outbuildings. As she looked, a woman followed by a small boy came out the front door of the cabin. The woman carried a spade. They walked to a big elm tree by a paling-fenced garden. The woman spent several minutes selecting a spot, then drove the spade in the ground with her foot. Instead of lifting a shovel of dirt she dropped to her knees and clasped the handle with both hands. The boy joined her. After several minutes, they stood, the woman wiped her eyes with her apron. She started digging.

Myra Belle frowned as she watched the woman work. She was digging an oblong hole.

The boy looked up and saw Myra Belle across the field. He screamed, "My God, maw, they are coming back!" The woman looked, then grabbed the boy's arm and pulled him as she ran toward the woods.

They thought she was a man. She pulled off her hat and fluffed her hair as she kicked Sambo into a run after the pair. She raced between them and the woods and then pulled up. "Don't be frightened. I mean you no harm."

The frightened woman gasped. "You-you are a girl!"

"Ma'am, who died and why are you so scared?" Myra Belle asked.

"He-he didn't die. They killed him." The woman stammered.

Myra Belle swung from her saddle. "Who killed who?"

"The Feds killed my husband." Myra Belle gripped the woman's arm. "When did the damned bluebellies kill your man?" The woman stepped back. She didn't believe it. The cold voice and tough language coming from such a young girl frightened her.

Myra Belle read the woman's thoughts and softened her voice. "I'm a friend. Tell me what happened."

Tears welled up in the woman's eyes. She brushed them back. "Seven or eight rode up here yesterday. My Jim was lying in the bed. He was hurt bad. Got shot in the chest at Carthage."

"Shot at Carthage?" Myra Belle put in.

"Yes, he rode with Ed Shirley. Ed was killed. My Jim was hit bad, but somehow he made it home on his horse. He was going to get well. I know it. I was caring for him and praying. Then yesterday the Feds came. They were here before I knew it. Didn't knock or anything, just busted in. An officer walked over to the bed, pulled back the covers and said, 'That's him.' "

The woman brushed back more tears. "Then the officer said, 'Take him outside.' I begged and pleaded, but they wouldn't listen. My Jim was near unconscious, couldn't fight. I grabbed my butcher knife and tried to fight." She paused and put her arm around the boy. "That officer said if I didn't stop, they—they would kill Joey. Then they took my Jim outside, shot him in the head and rode off." She broke into heavy sobs.

Myra Belle put an arm across the woman's shoulders. "Buck up, woman. We can't wilt to them damned Yankees. We have got to fight back. Get revenge. Ed Shirley was my brother."

The woman looked up. "You are Ed Shirley's little sister?"

"Yes, ma'am."

"Then you must be Myra Belle."

"How did you know my name?"

"Ed hid out here with us a lot. He liked to talk about you and the rest of his family. Your father is a judge."

"You must be Jim Moss's wife. Ed spoke of you." Myra Belle stepped back, her eyes flashing. "Mrs. Moss, I'm going to get even with those bluebellies if it's the last thing I do on earth." She paused. "Talking won't do it. Come on, let's bury your husband."

Myra Belle took the spade. Mrs. Moss and the boy watched, astonished at the slender girl's strength. When the grave was complete, the two women carried the blanket-wrapped body from the cabin, placing it in the grave.

Myra Belle filled the grave. While she worked Mrs. Moss went to the cabin and returned with a Bible. When the grave was rounded and packed she handed the worn book to Myra Belle. "I'm sure you can read. I can't. Jim always read the Good Book to me and Joey. It was something about 'the Lord is my Shepherd.' Would you read it over my Jim?"

"Sure." Myra Belle took the Bible and thumbed to the Twenty-third Psalm. She knew the passage well, but pretended to read. She asked Mrs. Moss and Joey to repeat it with her. After the brief service she asked, "Mrs. Moss, do you have any food in the house? I'm hungry. And do you have anything I can feed my horse?"

"All we have is a little piece of salt pork and some corn meal. We do have about a peck of shelled corn you can have for your horse."

Myra Belle fed and watered Sambo while Mrs. Moss fried some strips of pork and made some corn dodgers. After the meal Myra Belle asked, "Mrs. Moss, do you have a horse?"

"Yes, Jim's horse is hid back in the woods."

"You go get the horse. Then you take Joey and ride to Carthage. You can't stay here. You will be killed. The woods are full of Jayhawkers, Feds and bushwhackers. Believe me, ma'am, the whole state of Missouri is just one big battlefield." Myra Belle took a twenty-dollar gold piece from her pocket. "Take this. It will help to tide you over."

Mrs. Moss looked at her feet then up at Myra Belle. "I know you mean well, Miss Shirley, but I can't leave my Jim. I can't. I can't. This is our home." She broke into heavy sobs.

The sobbing irritated Myra Belle. She grabbed

Mrs. Moss by the shoulders. "Listen, woman, stop that bawling. There is a war going on. This is no time to be sentimental. Now, do what I say. Take your boy and get out of here."

Mrs. Moss shrank back. Myra Belle shook her. "Dammit, we haven't got all day. Go get that horse. I'm going to pack you up and get you started."

The cowed, frightened woman ran for the door. In a few minutes she returned with the horse. Myra Belle tied some blankets behind the saddle, then helped the woman and the boy mount up. Mrs. Moss started sobbing again. Myra Belle shouted, "Shut up and get going."

"I can't. I can't," the woman sobbed. Myra Belle didn't reply. Instead she slapped the horse's rump with a broom. He jumped into a fast gallop, almost unseating the riders. "Goodbye, Mrs. Moss. And don't you come back until this war is over."

Mrs. Moss's sobs carried back until she crossed the draw.

Myra Belle clenched her fists. "Women, weak damned women, why couldn't they stand up and fight like a man?" she shouted. "I will. I'm not afraid. I'll show those Feds just how a woman can fight."

Myra Belle stared after the Mosses several minutes, then rolled the balance of the salt pork in a cloth and tied it behind her saddle. She mounted Sambo and started to ride off, but pulled up and thought a moment. No, she wouldn't leave the Feds or Jayhawkers any plunder. Jumping from her horse she went into the house and tied some rags around the broom handle. She lit the handmade torch in the smoldering fireplace. When it was ablaze she fired the cabin, then ran and tossed the torch into the barn.

She rode a short distance, stopped and watched the cabin and barn go up in flames. What a waste wars were. Why did men want to kill and destroy? Now, she was a woman with the same lust. Yet, she consoled. *I have a reason—to revenge my brother.*

The Union Cavalry had about a four-hour start, Myra Belle guessed as she picked up their trail on the main road. She hadn't expected to kill so much time when she stopped at the Moss place. The time-span between her and the Union troops needed to be cut to about an hour, so she let Sambo into a long lope.

Her thoughts jumped about as she rode. A picture formed of the Union major she had met the evening before in camp. Was he the officer who dragged Jim Moss from his bed and shot him? The thought filled her mind with a searing hate.

It didn't take Sambo long to gain on the Feds. Soon a cloud of dust in front told Myra Belle the Union Cavalry was just ahead. She slowed Sambo to a walk. *Now just lay back and follow. Just keep them in sight and bide time.*

The dust, heat and August sun didn't tire the girl. Her emotions drove her on. Neither did she worry about tiring Sambo. He was some of the best horseflesh on the frontier. The cavalry quit the main road and turned east on a rough wagon road. It was actually a trail that snaked through heavy timber and rough boulders.

The rumor was correct. Turning east meant they were headed for Arkansas. The cavalry traveled carelessly, feeling so secure they didn't post rear guards. Myra Belle trailed a safe distance behind. The Feds knew there were no Confederate troops within miles. Yet, they didn't know they were being stalked by a much deadlier enemy—a revenge-crazed girl.

Late in the afternoon the road made a junction with the Independence-Fort Smith road. Myra Belle was sure they were now over the line in Arkansas. The cloud of dust stopped moving. The Feds were stopping to make a night camp.

Myra Belle rode into the brush and dismounted. Tying Sambo to a tree she slipped toward the sound of the troops. She wanted to be sure if they were making camp or just resting. At the top of a rise she dropped to her hands and knees, crawling behind some boulders. Peering through an opening between the rocks she could see the troops milling around in a little valley below.

There was something strange going on. A camp was already set up. She had stumbled on to an established, hidden Union rest camp. Mess and hospital tents were set off to one side, and several supply wagons were parked in a circle. Behind the wagons were some pole corrals holding horses and mules.

Excitement stormed over Myra Belle. This was big. The camp would be a "sitting duck" for a guerrilla raid. But there was more work to be done. Her brother Ed had been a good teacher. He had told her that before a successful raid against a superior force could be carried out there had to be a very accurate and detailed scouting report. This would be her job. Slipping through the rough ground she circled the camp, making mental notes on the number of men, wagons, horses and the locations of guards. Once she crawled within a few feet of a sentry. She pulled one of her guns and aimed it at the unsuspecting guard's head. The desire was hot, but she had no intention of pulling the trigger. A shot would bring a swarm of Feds. She wasn't afraid she couldn't escape on Sambo, but her plans would be wrecked. One dead bluebelly wasn't enough. She wanted many to die.

Darkness was falling when she finished her scouting and returned to her horse. She had to make a decision. It was about forty miles to the guerrilla camp in the Indian Territory. Should she ride through the night and try to find it, or wait until morning? Her mind fought back and forth. Time was important. The Feds might break camp and leave. Then there was the chance of getting lost in the darkness.

"What do you want to do, Sambo?"

Hearing his name the big stallion jerked at his tie rope. "You want action, don't you, boy? You're a real fighter." That was the answer. She untied the horse and plunged into the darkness.

Myra Belle studied the stars as she followed the rough trails in the darkness. She kept a north by west direction. She came to a trail following the Cowskin River. This was the trail she was looking for. This was the one her brother talked of in describing directions to the guerrilla camp.

The going was slow in the darkness. For the next several hours she followed the river trail. It was rough, but Sambo was sure-footed. She didn't worry about him stumbling. Wilderness night sounds were all about: the cry of bobcats, timber wolves' yelps and night birds fluttering in the trees. Instead of being frightened Myra Belle enjoyed the sounds of nature's free creatures. They fought for their own survival. She identified with them.

At dawn she found a slope on the steep riverbank. Dismounting she led Sambo down to the rushing cold mountain stream. While he drank she washed her face. The cold water cleared the cobwebs from her sleepy eyes. Nearby was a little sandy beach. She unsaddled Sambo, let him roll in the damp sand, then rubbed him down with a willow branch. After the rubdown she took a small bag of corn from her saddle.

Sambo whinnied at the sight of the food. She slapped his nose. "No, no, you know better than that." Dumping the corn in her hat she set it on the ground. Sambo ate as she chewed some of the salt pork and ate a corn dodger. While eating she thought of the experience with Mrs. Moss. Why were women weak? She thought of other weak women. The spineless Jayhawker heifers who submitted to rape, without a fight, while their men were being slaughtered. Oh, how she would have loved to witness the bloody butchery of pleading, dying Yankees. But those women, why didn't they fight? The thought was enraging. She jumped to her feet and clenched her fists. "No, no, I'm not weak. I'm tough, strong and I'll show the world a woman can fight," she said aloud.

Myra Belle shook her head. She must control her emotions. If not, she would be like other women. No, it would never happen again. Sambo had finished his corn and was nipping at some tender grass. She saddled him and hit the trail. Riding slowly and studying her surroundings, she fit them into the description her brother had given her. She was in the vicinity of the guerrilla camp. There were the odd-shaped bluffs on the opposite river bank that Ed had described in detail, even mentioning a small waterfall spouting from a crevice.

A flash of brilliant color flipped from between the bluffs. Myra Belle pulled up. She whipped one of the big revolvers from its holster. She stared hard.

Then a relaxed smile spread across her face. It was the waterfall. The rising sun hitting the spilling water was creating a rainbow. Downstream she saw the other landmark Ed had spoken of, a shallow ford across the river.

Her mind worked. Across the ford was a trail.

"Hold it right there! And get your hands up!" a rough voice ordered.

Myra Belle raised her hands and turned in the saddle. She was neither frightened, nor startled. She was expecting the challenge. She would have been disappointed in the guerrillas' security if they had not posted guards. It made her proud. They weren't careless. The brush parted and a man rode out, rifle leveled. It was Arch Thomas, a carpenter from Carthage. "Why, Mr. Thomas, I'm Myra Belle Shirley."

Thomas blinked his eyes. "I'm a son of a gun. What on earth are you doing out here?"

"I've come here to join your band and fight."

"Myra Belle Shirley, your folks wouldn't allow such a thing. They are probably worried sick about you. No doubt you have run away. Now turn that horse around and get back home."

"No! I want to see your leader."

"Look, Myra Belle, you don't understand. We are a rough crowd. We are all wanted, desperate men, dedicated to die for a cause we believe is right, just like your brother Ed." Thomas inched closer as he talked. "Please, now listen to me and go home." His hand shot out and grabbed Sambo's bridle. "And if you don't go, I'll hogtie you and carry you home."

It happened quickly. Thomas was looking in the muzzles of the big forty-fours. "Take me to your leader, Mr. Thomas. I mean it. I have some very important business to discuss with him." Thomas was not looking at the leveled guns, but beyond. It was those piercing cold black eyes. The message was there. "All right, but lower those guns."

Thomas headed his horse across the stream, with Myra Belle following. They picked up a trail that wound through a slit in the bluffs into a small meadow. Across the meadow the trail dodged through some heavy timber and big boulders, leading to the top of a steep ridge. Myra Belle turned in her saddle. "Mr. Thomas, who is your leader? Do I know him?"

"No, I don't think so. His name's Anderson."

"Bill Anderson?"

"Yes, know him?"

"I have never met him, but I've heard of him. He's real tough."

The conversation was interrupted. "Who goes there?" a voice challenged from behind a boulder.

"Arch Thomas, I'm coming in."

"Go ahead, Arch. But whoa, who's that with you?"

"Never mind, someone to see Bill."

They rode through a passage in the boulders into a clearing. Myra Belle surveyed the layout. The place was a natural fortress surrounded by huge trees and rocks. On one corner were some ledges forming a large shallow cave. The camp was just waking up. Men were moving about. Some were around a small fire drinking coffee from tin cups. Thomas led the way over to the men by the fire. One man looked up. "Arch, where did you get that kid?"

Thomas didn't answer the question. Instead he asked, "Is Bill up?"

None of the men had recognized Myra Belle as a girl. "Yeah, Bill is up. Just got a cup of coffee and went back to his bedroll over there under the cliff."

Myra Belle followed Thomas across the clearing. She could see a big whiskered man crouched under one of the ledges. As they neared he stood and stared hard at the pair. "Who you got with you, Arch?" The voice was gruff.

Myra Belle didn't let Thomas answer. "I'm Myra Belle Shirley, Ed's sister. Are you Bill Anderson?"

"So you are the kid sister Ed was always talking about." Then his face hardened even more. "All right, young lady, what do you want?" He stepped closer. "Speak up. Then Arch will escort you out of here. This is no place for a lady."

Myra Belle boiled. *No place for a woman.* Everyone had the same opinion of women, as spineless and helpless. *Cut it out. Show them women have guts,* a voice inside her said. The anger was replaced by a tinge of excitement. She was face to face with Bloody Bill Anderson. He was the most ruthless of all the guerrillas. A bloodthirsty, vicious killer, who preferred cutting throats to shooting. "Speak up, girl," Anderson commanded again.

"I want to speak to you in private, Mr. Anderson."

The guerrilla leader glared. "All right, since you're here, get off your horse." He turned to Thomas. "Hold her horse and wait, Arch."

Myra Belle dismounted and followed Anderson in under the cliff. He pointed to a bedroll atop some other gear. "Have a seat." It was a command, not an invitation. She squatted on the bedroll. He sat down on a wooden box facing her. "Tell me your story, I'm a busy man."

Bloody Bill listened as Myra Belle gave a detailed account of the Yankee troop movements. To her surprise when she finished he pulled a Bowie knife from his belt and patted his knee with the flat side of the blade. "Miss Shirley, I believe you have turned Yankee spy and are trying to lead us into a —."

He didn't finish. He was staring into the muzzle of a big forty-four. "Mr. Anderson, no one calls me a Yankee. I'll kill you. I don't give a damn who you are. One move with that knife and you are dead, understand?"

Their stares locked. Bloody Bill lost to those piercing black eyes. He had cowed, raped, even murdered women. But now he was facing a young she-devil. "Apologize, Mr. Anderson, or I'll kill you. Then I'll go after those damned Yankees myself. They killed my brother. I won't be cheated out of my revenge."

Anderson took a deep breath. He wasn't afraid of man or beast, but this girl was different. Yes, she would kill him. For the first time in his life he was going to apologize. "Miss Shirley, I'm sorry. Understand, our very lives depend on us being careful and suspicious. And for a young girl to ride in here and tell the story you did is hard to believe. But I believe you."

"Thank you, I accept your apology. Now are you interested in a plan I have?"

"Yes, let's hear it, but first put that gun up." He stuck his knife back in his belt. "You are as fast with a gun as your brother said you were, faster than most men." He turned and walked to the front of the cave. "Arch, put up Miss Shirley's horse. I'll talk to you later."

Myra Belle again detailed the Feds' camp and how easy it would be to raid. When she finished, Anderson walked in small circles in deep thought for several minutes, stopped, turned. "You must be exhausted. Take my bedroll and get back there in the corner and get some sleep. We are going to ride tonight. There will be a guard posted outside." He turned and walked toward the men by the fire.

Myra Belle unrolled the blankets and stretched out. Even though dog-tired, she was too excited to sleep. Bloody Bill Anderson was going to hit the Union Troops. And she was going to get revenge. Many years later Belle said that meeting and being accepted by Bill Anderson was the biggest thrill of her life.

Fatigue overcame excitement and the young woman slept. Late in the afternoon she was awakened by Anderson's gruff voice. "Wake up, Little Reb. It will soon be time to ride."

She brushed the sleep from her eyes and walked from under the ledge. Men were milling about, some already mounted, others making ready. Bill Anderson was sitting astride a big sorrel, holding Sambo. He pitched her the reins. "Mount up, Little Reb, and follow me."

They headed out through the passage, Bloody Bill in the lead, Myra Belle close behind. She looked back over her shoulder and counted the riders, twenty-seven dirty, scraggly, but savage and ruthless fighters riding to attack several hundred trained troops.

The band headed up the river trail. At the junction of the trail and wagon road Anderson held up his hand signaling a stop. He stood high in his stirrups and whistled, shrill and loud. The whistle echoed through the rough country. It was not an ordinary whistle, but the cry of a bird. In a few seconds an answering call came from the woods. Myra Belle was fascinated with the signals and wondered who Anderson was communicating with. He read her thoughts. "We are going to be joined by a Cherokee I sent for. He knows this country like the back of his hand."

In a few minutes the brush parted and a rider emerged. Myra Belle's eyes widened. She expected anything except what she saw. The rider was a misfit, looking out of place with the rest of the band. Young, handsome, dressed in a Confederate officer's uniform, he sat tall in the saddle with an aristocratic haughtiness. "Captain Sam Starr, meet Miss Myra Shirley, Ed's sister," Anderson said.

Starr touched his hat. "The pleasure is mine, Miss Shirley." A strange buzz of excitement stung Myra Belle. She noticed the captain looked no older than she.

At Anderson's request Myra Belle gave Starr a detailed briefing of her scouting report. He listened in silence, occasionally nodding. "Very good, I can find them. But if you can backtrack your trail in the darkness it will save time. Can you?" Myra Belle was amazed at the Cherokee's good English.

"Yes, sir, I'm sure I can, Captain Starr."

Starr turned to Anderson. "Let's ride."

Darkness soon draped over the rough country. Myra Belle rode the lead, followed by Starr, then Anderson. She strained her eyes in full concentration on the trail, watching for landmarks by the pale moonlight. They rode hard, never stopping for a rest. Lesser horses would have tired, but the guerrillas were well mounted. The band rode in silence, dark shadows moving along the wooded hills.

Myra Belle had a strange strong feeling. Captain Starr and Anderson had confidence in her. She wondered about Sam Starr. His speech said he was educated and he was so different from the few other

Indians she had met. Why was he riding with the guerrillas?

After several hours they broke from the back trails on to the wagon road Myra Belle and the Union Cavalry had traveled the day before. She pulled up. It was still about an hour before dawn. "The camp is over the next ridge. About a mile, I guess," she said in a low voice.

Anderson turned to the rider behind him. "Pass it back. We're stopping for awhile. Everyone dismount." Saddle leather creaked and gear rattled as the tired men swung to the ground.

"Captain Starr, you go ahead and scout the camp. Make it as quick as possible."

Myra Belle watched with interest as Starr turned sideways in his saddle and pulled off his boots. Then he took a pair of moccasins from his saddlebags and slipped them on. He jumped to the ground and pitched her his reins. "Look after my horse until I get back." Not a twig snapped as he vanished into the dense forest.

The men and horses stamped about nervously, but there was no conversation. Excitement was clutching Myra Belle. It was going to happen. Nothing else mattered. Her tormented mind screamed, "Kill! Kill! Blood! Revenge!" Waiting for Starr to return made her edgy. Minutes seemed hours.

Just as silently as he disappeared, Starr emerged from the brush. He and Anderson walked off to one side and held a whispered conference. Then Anderson turned to the men. "Gather around."

"Just over the next ridge is our destination, a big Union encampment." He paused. This was the first time Myra Belle realized the men didn't know their mission. The guerrilla leader continued: "They are about three-hundred strong. We are going to slip to the top of the hill. Then when I give the command, we hit them." He paused again. "We ride in fast and loud. The damned bluebellies will run like rabbits. Shoot everything that moves except the horses. We want them and the supply wagons. Every man knows his job. And we must get in and out fast. Now, mount up and we ride."

At dawn the band hid in the brush atop the ridge. Below, the unsuspecting Union troops were just beginning to stir. Myra Belle could hear her own rapid heartbeat. On all sides the raiders were inspecting their guns. She took her guns from their holsters and rotated the cylinders. They felt good in her hands. Then came the bitter disappointment. Bloody Bill moved over to her. "Miss Shirley, you're staying here."

Her face went white in disbelief, then flushed with anger. "No," she snapped.

His voice cut like a knife. "I give the orders, get it? You stay here."

Myra Belle fought back her anger. This wasn't the time to argue, or make a scene. "Yes sir," she muttered. She looked at Captain Starr. He was staring at the camp below, his handsome face emotionless, the gray officer's hat pulled low over his eyes and a gun in each hand. She wondered why he hated Yankees.

Bloody Bill raised his hand, paused and seemed to count under his breath. Then his hand swept downward as he spurred his horse. The guerrillas broke from the woods in a yelling wave—a small dedicated band attacking an army. Then the raiders were upon the startled Union troops.

Myra Belle jumped from her horse, stomped,

clapped, yelling "Kill, kill!" as the guerrillas tore into the helpless soldiers. An early mess line in front of a tent was hit first. Most were shot in their tracks. Two tried to run for the cover of the woods. They were run down. Then the raiders ran their horses back and forth through the half-asleep soldiers still rolled in their blankets. The ones not shot were trampled.

The major in charge dashed from his tent half-dressed with a saber in his hand. He tried to shout orders. Seeing the officer, Bloody Bill and Sam Starr whirled their horses toward him. Anderson waved Starr back. Then jumped from his horse with the big Bowie knife in his hand facing the officer with the saber. Anderson moved forward in a crouch. The major slashed with the saber. Bloody Bill ducked the blade. Then with one rip the major's bowels spilled over his belt. As the wounded man staggered backward another slash cut his throat. Myra Belle screamed in fiendish delight. It was happening. She was seeing it. No dream, all was real—damned Yankees dying like dogs, groaning, even some on their knees praying, pleading, then dying, damn them.

The massacre was brief, bloody and thorough. The guerrillas rounded up the Union horses and three supply wagons loaded with food, guns and clothing. Then they fired the camp. None of the raiders suffered so much as a scratch. Myra Belle rode at the side of Bloody Bill as the band headed for the Indian Territory with their booty. She felt a slight disappointment. Captain Starr didn't return with them. After the fight, he waved and vanished into the woods. This was the only time Myra Belle saw Sam Starr for many years.

The trip back to the camp was slow, because of

the captured wagons. Even though exhausted, the men were in high spirits. Most changed horses and rode the captured cavalry mounts. It was after midnight when they reached their base.

The men dismounted, took care of their horses, then turned their attention to the supply wagons. They surrounded the one which carried several barrels of sugar. The barrels were broken open with an axe and the men swarmed on the sugar like vultures, gulping handfuls with childish lip-smacking.

Myra Belle watched with interest. She had never witnessed people satisfying a starved taste before. Hungry humans were like dogs, she thought. Bloody Bill rode over to her. His clothes were still stained with the Union major's blood. "Let me have your horse. You go sleep in my quarters again. I will talk to you tomorrow."

She dismounted and started to walk away when one of the men left the crowd and grabbed her arm. Before she could react, Bloody Bill was on the man, clubbing him to the ground with the butt of a revolver. "You dog," he said and kicked the fallen man. Then he said to Myra Belle, "Hurry up. You'll be guarded the rest of the night."

Myra Belle replied. "I can take care of myself."

"Not here you can't. Now shut up, and get the hell to bed."

She fought back the resentment of being ordered around and walked to the shallow cave. The past two days swirled through her mind as she stretched her tired body on the bedroll. It was done. It was sweet. Now the future, what? She tried to think, but her mind wouldn't focus. The excitement was being replaced by exhaustion. Without any fear of the men outside she slept.

The sun was at midmorning when Myra Belle

came awake. She slipped on her boots and walked to the front of the cave. Bloody Bill was hunkered against a boulder, the Bowie knife in one hand. He was half asleep, but heard her stirring and sprang to his feet. His sleepless eyes were narrow blood-shot slits. "Oh, it's you." He stuck the big knife in his belt. "You hungry?"

At the mention of food she realized she hadn't eaten in over twenty-four hours. "Yes, sir."

"I'll go bring some food and coffee; we will talk while we eat."

In a few minutes he returned with two tin plates piled with grits, salt pork, corn dodgers and two cups of coffee. Myra Belle took a plate and sat cross-legged on a box. Bloody Bill pulled up another box. "Miss Shirley, you are as dedicated to this cause as I am."

She swallowed a bit. "Yes, sir."

Instead of continuing the conversation he got up and walked to the front of the opening. After staring outside for several minutes he returned. "You want to continue to fight for our cause?"

"Yessir, I want to join you."

The guerrilla leader leaned forward. "Little lady, and you are a lady—I know your background, your breeding and family. I admire your guts. Even though you are no more than a child, you are the most unusual woman I've ever met. I never thought I would run into a female with your spunk and brains." He kicked at the dirt searching for words. "However, with all your sense, you are ignorant of the world. There are things you aren't old enough to understand. If you stayed here it would be like throwing raw meat to a gang of wolves."

He swept his arm toward the front of the cave. "Those men out there are animals, only more vicious. I'm an animal. Guarding you last night was the first human thing I've done in years." He leaned closer. "It hasn't occured to you, that last night I thought of taking you first, then turning you over to that pack."

"This will surprise you, Mr. Anderson, it did. But I knew I could trust you." She patted the big guns. "And these."

His eyes showed surprise. A brief softness crossed his hard features. "Trust, don't depend on it if you want to stay alive. Do you know I trust few of those men out there who would follow me to hell. At least half of them aren't loyal to the cause, or any other cause, except their bellies, greed and the thrill of raiding. Do you know why they joined up with me?"

"No, sir."

"Just like any other animal, they joined the pack to survive."

Myra Belle looked outside at the men and nodded.

Taking the Bowie knife from his belt, Bloody Bill whetted it on his boot leg, then raised his eyes and stared straight at Myra Belle. "Last night while guarding you, I fought two battles with myself. The one with lust I told you about. The other: whether to let you ride out of here, or not. You could be caught and intimidated by the Yankees into giving them our location. Yes, if they find out about your part in the raid, you are a dead woman. By holding a death warrant over your head they could make you talk. You are now wanted—a traitor against the United States of America, understand?"

Myra Belle matched Bloody Bill's stare. "I understand, and did before I came to you. To hell with the Yankees. And I told you yesterday never to call me a traitor against our cause."

"I didn't."

"No, but you are insinuating that I'm a weak, spineless women that would turn tail to save her hide. Never, never. If you don't want me I'll fight by myself."

The guerrilla leader stood. "You have convinced me. And I may have plans for you. You can be very valuable to our cause. But first, I want to get one thing straight."

"What?"

"You are a very headstrong person. Will you, and can you take orders?"

The pointblank question caught Myra Belle by surprise. An odd flair of temper, maybe resentment, boiled up. Here was a man wanting to give her orders. She had always taken orders and obeyed her father until the day she had ridden away. But that was different. Did Anderson still consider her a weak female too foolish to take care of herself? She fought it off. "Yes, sir, I will."

"All right, you go back home to Carthage and be a nice little schoolgirl. Keep your eyes and ears open. You will be contacted by one of my men. What we are looking for are small isolated units, like the one you led us to. There are many such units in Southeastern Missouri."

CHAPTER THREE

John Shirley was standing in front of his hotel when Myra Belle rode in. He ran to meet her. "Thank God! You're back and safe."

There was a tearful reunion between the girl and her parents. "Where have you been, Myra Belle? And I pray to God you didn't do what you threatened," Shirley asked.

"I've just been riding around. No, I didn't kill anyone." Her voice carried a ring of disappointment.

Next morning Myra Belle started for school as if nothing had happened. A few days later on her way home a young man stepped from an alley and called in a low voice, "Miss Shirley."

She was startled, but not frightened. How did the stranger know her name? Was he the contact Bloody Bill Anderson promised? Or was the man a Yankee undercover agent? Then she looked closer at the stranger and almost laughed at her thoughts. He wasn't a man, but a kid, no older or larger than she. "Yes, I'm Myra Belle Shirley, what do you want?"

He moved closer and said, "Pleased to meet you. My name is Jim Dancer. Bill Anderson sent me to work with you. We can't talk here. When and where can we meet?"

Myra Belle could hardly believe Anderson would

41

send such a youngster. Was someone trying to entrap her? She would find out, play the game. "Tonight, out back of my father's livery stable, meet me at nine o'clock."

Because of her fondness for horses, the Shirleys weren't suspicious when Myra Belle said she was going out to check the horses. Dancer was waiting and got down to business. "You don't know me and you are suspicious, aren't you, Miss Shirley?"

"Not exactly suspicious, just careful." She patted one of the big revolvers under her blouse.

"You're as tough as Anderson said," Dancer observed, and took a folded paper from his shirt pocket. "I'll light a match, you read."

By the feeble light of the sulphur match she read the short note. "Jim, Carthage may be the end. If it is, join up with Bill Anderson. You are the best spy in the country. He can use you. The fight must go on. Your friend, Ed Shirley."

Myra Belle blinked. There was no doubt. It was her brother's writing. "All right, I trust you," she said and handed back the note.

Dancer stuck the match to the paper. "It wouldn't be good if Union troops found that in our possession."

Myra Belle stared hard as the note crumpled into ashes. She would have liked to keep it, but Dancer was right. "That is why I'm fighting, Jim."

"We all have our reasons, Myra Belle. Now quickly I must tell you our plans. Then I must go. I'm much older than I look, twenty-two. I pose as an orphan and hang around Union camps, begging for food, shining their boots and taking their abuse. They don't suspect I'm mentally recording their every action, then passing it on to Quantrill and Anderson."

Myra Belle cut in. "Where do I fit in?"

"You are to ride around the countryside, visit Union camps as if you are a curious young lady and gather information—just like I'm doing. Then we meet every few days, you give me what you have learned and I pass it to the right people."

Myra liked the plan except the last part. Again she wasn't being trusted because she was a woman. She had to give the information to Dancer and let him pass it on. Why couldn't she deliver it first-hand? Her temper started to flare. But she caught it. She had promised Anderson to take orders. "Where and how will I find you when I have some information?" she asked.

"I'll find you. Don't worry. And good luck," Dancer replied, then walked into the darkness.

Myra Belle followed orders; dressed in a riding skirt, riding sidesaddle, she posed as a timid young lady. She encountered no problems riding into the Union camps. The homesick soldiers were always eager to admit a pretty young lady and make conversation. The officers pushed ahead of the soldiers for the opportunity to visit with the dainty visitor. Her conversation seemed to be that of a curious, not-quite-grown-up girl. None suspected they were supplying one of their deadliest and craftiest enemies with information that might lead to their deaths.

For many months Myra Belle worked with Jim Dancer. She admired his guts and brains and studied his tactics. He controlled his emotions—always in control, never moved until he had every detail and the upper hand.

The information the spy team supplied led to countless raids on small, isolated Union detachments by guerrilla bands. On several occasions

Myra Belle hid and watched the attacks with satisfaction.

She kept her spy activities so well concealed she wasn't even suspected by her parents. But someone may have had a suspicion of Myra Belle. One day while she was at school Union troops rode to the Shirley place and burned the hotel and stables.

Myra Belle was furious. She jumped on a horse and rode to Jim Dancer's hideout—an abandoned shack on the outskirts of Carthage. When she entered, Dancer grabbed her shoulders and pushed her against a wall. "Dammit, I told you never to ride a horse in here during daylight. Quick, what's up? Then you get the hell out of here."

"Jim, I know what you said. I'm sorry, but you don't understand. The damned Yankees have burned us out—hotel and everything."

Dancer stepped back and released his grip on her shoulders. "Jayhawkers, or Union troops?"

"Father said Union troops."

"How many? And did he know which outfit?"

"There were only eight, but he wouldn't know which outfit like you and I would."

Dancer shook his head. "Maybe they are wise to you. No, or they would have gone to the school and got you. But they had a reason to single out your folks."

"Jim, we have to get them."

"Maybe, you see if you can find out which outfit and I'll talk to some people tonight. I'll meet you tomorrow about four after school, down by the creek. Now, get out of here. And don't you ever ride in—" The sound of approaching hoofbeats cut him off. He ran to the door. "Dammit, here comes a Yankee officer. Followed you probably."

Myra Belle whipped one of the big forty-fours

from under her blouse. Dancer grabbed her arm. "Put that up and stay out of sight. I'll handle this. One shot and the whole Union army will be down on us."

Dancer walked outside. Myra Belle boiled; being pushed around by a man again. But she cooled, Dancer was right. She was learning—getting lessons from a professional. She heard the officer's voice. "Kid, who are you? And where did you get that fine horse?"

Dancer replied, "Name's Joe Smith, horse belongs to my paw, he's in the Union army."

Leather squeaked and Myra Belle knew the officer was dismounting. "Kid, you are a damned Rebel liar. Your name isn't Joe Smith and your paw isn't in the Union army. Probably a damned bushwhacker. And that horse belongs to Judge Shirley. I trailed his daughter here. The little wench is up to something. And Joe Smith, you are going to tell me what."

"I don't know what you're talking about, sir."

"Come here, boy. Don't try to run or I'll shoot you," the officer said and then laughed. "I love to shoot Rebels."

Myra Belle could stand the suspense no longer. Union army or not she was going to shoot the Yankee officer to save her friend, Dancer. She went to the door, the big forty-four leveled. The officer, a big man, was advancing on Dancer, his fists balled. "Talk up, Reb, or I'm going to beat you to death."

Dancer was slowly back-pedaling. "No, no sir, I don't know no Shirley girl." Myra Belle was disappointed. She thought Dancer was tough. And here he was whimpering like a coward. The officer moved forward, Dancer backward. Then he was cornered. He had backed into the officer's horse. The officer slowed and laughed. "Hemmed yourself in, didn't you, Reb?" He cocked his fists.

"Talk up, Reb, or get both of these right in your teeth." The officer taunted raising his fists. Then there was a blur of movement. Myra Belle saw something flash in the sunlight, the officer screamed and staggered backward, half his face gone. Dancer had intentionally backed into the officer's horse and jerked the saber from its holder. Now Dancer had the handle of the saber in both hands, and he swung it like an axe. The officer's head jumped from its body, landing several feet away in some weeds. As the headless body thrashed in a bloody circle on the ground, Myra Belle ran and kicked it. "Die, damn you, die!" she shouted.

Dancer jammed the saber through the lifeless body, pinning it to the ground, then he turned to Myra Belle standing wide eyed. "You enjoyed that."

Yes, she enjoyed the blood-spraying body thrashing its life away and the head rolling into the weeds, gasping. A strange fierceness was stinging her every fiber, uncontrollably. She lunged forward, arms wide. "Please, Jim, please," she screamed. They clinched, two wild things tearing at each other. Their lips pressed together, sucking and nibbling as they tumbled on the bloodstained grass near the body. Dancer's hands fondled as they moved down between her thighs.

They rolled, his hands tugging at her clothes. She helped, raising her thighs and kicking one leg free of her jeans. Inflamed, she pulled him down upon her. "Now, now," she whispered. They locked, savage, sweating and panting. Teeth nipped, hot tongues licked, fingers ripped and clawed as wave after wave of wild nature forced total exertion.

Their breath and strength seeped back. Dancer

rolled to one side and sat up. He looked at the headless body several seconds, then turned to Myra Belle, his face now stern. "The war, it's all over. We lost. You lost a brother. I lost my entire family. Maybe we evened the score. I don't know."

He stood and extended a hand to Myra Belle. They straightened their clothes. Dancer glanced at the body again. "As I said, it's all over, Myra Belle. You want to live, so do I. We will both carry scars, but what we just did won't be one. I'm heading out of here into the unknown, something better, I hope. You go home and try to put your life back together." He bent, kissed her, whirled and dashed in to the brush.

"Good luck, Jim," Myra Belle shouted, then mounted her horse. She spit at the face of the lifeless head as she stuck her heels to her horse.

CHAPTER FOUR

Myra Belle took Dancer's advice and went home. The Shirleys held a conference. John and Eliza Shirley were sick of war. Myra believed Dancer, that it was over and the South had lost. They decided to gather up what few assets they had left, move to Texas and join the older son, Preston. Unlike the other members of the Shirley family, Preston took little part in the war. Yet the Union classified him as a guerrilla. A warrant was issued for him and he fled to Texas for safety.

John Shirley was a tough man. He could get knocked down, then get up. His hard work, intelligence, and education gave him the ability to overcome adversities regardless of how rough. In Texas the Shirleys bought a large tract of land between Mesquite and Scyene, near Preston's place. Again the Shirleys turned to raising fine horses and prospered.

Just as in Missouri the family soon became prominent social and church leaders in the community. Myra Belle enrolled in a nearby advanced school and soon became the most popular young lady in the region.

Three happy prosperous years passed for the Shirleys. They all, including Myra Belle, seemed to have forgotten the war and readjusted. Myra Belle,

49

now eighteen, was the apple of all the bachelors' eyes. They came calling in droves. She was friendly, courteous to her many admirers, but that was all. When they tried to get serious she dropped them. Her interest was in school and helping her father with horse raising.

Then one summer evening Myra Belle, John and Eliza were sitting on the front porch of their home. They saw dust from a band of riders approaching. This wasn't unusual. But Myra Belle had a troubled feeling. Why were the riders traveling across open land and not following the road? She turned to her father. "Wonder who those riders are?"

"I don't know. Strange they are riding across country and not the road."

"I was thinking the same thing," Mrs. Shirley added.

John Shirley went in the house and returned with a rifle; he wanted to be prepared in case of trouble. The riders headed straight for the Shirley house and pulled to a halt at the front gate. Myra Belle counted eight. All were young, tough-looking and heavily armed. Their dirty clothes, sweaty faces and tired horses showed they had ridden far and hard.

John Shirley stepped from the porch, rifle ready. "What can I do for you gentlemen?"

One man stepped his horse forward. He was tall, broad-shouldered, with wide blue eyes. "Are you Judge John Shirley from Carthage, Missouri?"

The thought of carpetbaggers shot through Myra Belle's mind. She ran inside the house, and returning with a shotgun she joined her father. "Yes, I'm Judge Shirley. State your business, gentlemen." He cocked the rifle.

The big man swung from his saddle and opened the front yard gate. "That's far enough, mister. Answer my father, or eat lead," Myra Belle snapped.

The big man smiled. "I'm sorry, folks, we should have introduced ourselves. We're Missouri boys. I'm Cole Younger, the others are my brothers and some friends. We all rode with Quantrill and were friends of your son, Ed."

Myra Belle's heart fluttered—Quantrill, the raids, Ed's murder, then revenge, the sweet revenge. The fire rekindled.

John Shirley lowered the rifle then gripped the big hand Cole Younger extended. "Welcome, Mr. Younger, you and your friends must spend the night with us. Good ole Missouri boys are always welcome in the Shirley home."

While the men took care of the horses, Myra Belle and her mother prepared dinner for the guests. Myra Belle felt light and fierce. It was great to see some real men again—her kind of men, strong and tough.

With the horses cared for, the men washed up at the pump, then went to the barn and changed clothes. Myra Belle noted washing and clean clothes had done wonders. The ruffian look was gone, replaced by a wild, adventurous appearance. The kind of men to be admired. After dinner they moved to the front porch. Myra Belle made sure she found a seat by Cole Younger on the porch swing. John Shirley opened the conversation. "Well, boys, how is everything back in Missouri since the war?"

After a long silence, Cole Younger answered. "Mr. Shirley, it's bad. Not the same old Missouri you and I loved years ago. The damned Yankees have taken over. They control everything—banks, railroads, farms, political offices, everything. And anything they can't steal, they are legally foreclosing—land, businesses, livestock, even goats and pigs. You have a choice—either knuckle under or leave. We left."

One of the others cut in. "And if that isn't bad enough the Yankees are forcing people to sell the railroads' rights-of-ways for nothing."

Cole picked up the conversation again. "The real problem is, anyone who fought for, or sympathized with the Confederacy is open game. They will take your holdings and valuables, then kill you if you talk back. Murder and violence are still on the land."

Myra Belle listened with interest, the old hate boiling higher with every word. John Shirley cut in. "Hate to hear of all the trouble. We were planning on making a trip back to Missouri this fall. I wanted to see if we could recover some of our financial holdings."

Cole laughed. "Excuse me, sir; it isn't funny. But your chances of recovering anything would be as slim as finding a spring in a desert. No sir, you stay out of Missouri. Too many know you were on the Confederate side. As soon as you arrived you would be arrested on some trumped-up charge, maybe killed." He paused, then continued. "That is why we left. Our lives aren't worth two cents in Missouri. Maybe we can get a new start someplace."

John Shirley said, "You should be able to pick up the pieces and start over. You're young. And let me say, you boys are more than welcome to stay here with us until you figure out something."

"Thank you, Judge Shirley." Cole replied. Then the talk dwindled and everyone went to bed. Cole and his men took their bedrolls to the barn. Myra

Belle couldn't sleep. Cole Younger and his men hadn't been run out of Missouri. Of this she was certain. Their type didn't run, they fought. What was their game? Why were they in Texas? She would find out. Thinking of Cole Younger stirred excitement.

After breakfast all the men except Cole rode off, saying they were going to Dallas to look around. Myra Belle was delighted. She wanted to talk with Cole Younger alone. Soon after the others left she got her opportunity. Her father complained of not feeling well. So Myra Belle volunteered to go check some mares and colts in a back pasture. When she walked from the house Cole was sitting in the shade of a cottonwood, reading his Bible. "Mr. Younger, father isn't feeling well. And I must check some mares and colts. Would you mind giving me a hand?"

Cole lowered his Bible. "Why sure, Miss Shirley. Be more than glad to do something to earn my keep, since I'm going to be around a few days. I was just getting ready to ask your father if there was anything I could do." He stood and smiled. "And it will be a pleasure to work with a beautiful young lady."

The compliment sent a thrill through Myra Belle. It came from a real man. Suddenly the thrill turned to a strange excitement. She wanted Cole Younger. He was her kind of man. But first things first—she pushed back her emotions. Why was he in Texas? She must know.

They saddled and rode to the back pasture. After the horses were looked after, Myra Belle led the way to a spring surrounded by leafy cottonwoods. "Let's get a cool drink and rest a few minutes," she said. They turned their horses loose on the tender

grass, drank from the spring, then seated themselves in the shade facing each other.

"I'm glad you stopped by, Mr. Younger. It brings
back memories, some good, some bad."

Cole was studying Myra Belle. "Yes, and young
lady, you are just as pretty and spunky as your
brother Ed said you were. Also, I heard some great
things about you from Bill Anderson and Jim
Dancer. But you have sure grown up since those
days."

Myra Belle smiled. "I'm eighteen now." She
wanted him to know she was a woman. She fought
back her sexual excitement. That had to wait.
There were more important things. She looked him
straight in the eye. "It galls the hell out of me to
learn those damned Yankees are taking over Missouri. I can't figure you running out. You and your
friends just aren't the kind to turn tail."

Cole's big blue eyes sharpened. Myra Belle knew
she had scored. He plucked a blade of grass, chewed
it, then tossed it aside. "Yes, you are as sharp as
they said. You aren't fooled." He seemed to be talking to himself. "Bloody Bill and Dancer said you
were tough and could be trusted. I think you can
be."

Myra Belle cut in. "You can trust me."

Cole leaned forward. "We are down here in Texas
cooling off." He paused, still studying her and
debating with himself. "Myra Belle, you are correct. No, we aren't afraid of no damned Yankees.
Yes, we are fighting back, but in a different way
from what you knew."

"How?"

Cole stood, taking a leather pouch from inside his
shirt. He said, "We are robbing Yankee banks."
Myra Belle's eyes widened. Cole opened the bag

and shook several pieces of gold on the ground. "This is only a small amount of the loot we took from the Liberty Bank."

Myra Belle scooped up the gold. Tossing it from one hand to the other she shouted, "Gold! Gold! Damned Yankees' gold; you took it!" Then she sprang to her feet and threw her arms around Cole Younger. He fell backward. They rolled and caressed on the soft grass, lips and bodies locked. It was their world, Myra Belle Shirley's and Cole Younger. Then they were exhausted.

It was late afternoon when they rode home. They rode stirrup to stirrup. Myra Belle was in high delight. She had her kind of man. The excitement of lovemaking was dulling, but another fire was kindling in her mind. She turned her head toward Cole. "You are right. The way to even the score with the Yankees is to rob their banks."

Cole didn't answer, just nodded. Myra Belle's mind was now flaming. "Cole, I want to join you and help even the score with those damned Yankees."

Cole jerked erect in the saddle. "What?"

"I want to ride with you."

"A woman ride with us? Don't think you understand our activities."

She grabbed his bridle reins and jerked his horse to a stop. Her face flushed and her eyes sharpened: a man trying to belittle her. "A woman, eh? Hell, I can outride, outshoot and outtough you, or any man in your outfit."

Cole knew he was on the spot. Myra Belle had stirred something inside him more than his manhood. He wasn't sure if it was love or something else: maybe admiration. He did know she was beautiful and different from any woman he had ever met. He remembered Jim Dancer describing her as a "revenge-crazed little she-devil, but she could be trusted."

Cole fought to clear his mind. She was forcing him to make a decision he didn't want to make. He had no choice. Then maybe he did. "What about your folks? What will they think?" he asked.

"Let me take care of my folks. I said I wanted to ride with you and I won't take no for an answer."

"All right, little tiger, we ride out day after tomorrow, be ready."

Myra Belle smiled. "One thing more: I'm a big girl now. No more of that 'Myra Belle.' From now on my name is just Belle. And you can bet I'll be ready to ride."

Belle went to bed early but couldn't sleep. She lay awake, her mind a whirl of excitement and frustration. She couldn't wait to ride with the outlaws, but how would she tell her parents? She couldn't tell them she was hitting the outlaw trail. Sure, they hated Yankees, but breaking the law and robbing banks, no. And her riding off with a man, no, they wouldn't stand for that either. Her parents would want a wedding. She loved her parents deeply and didn't want to hurt them again.

Her mind fought back and forth. Maybe she should just forget Cole Younger and the whole deal. But that uncontrollable wish for revenge pushed her reasoning aside. "Go! Ride with the outlaws. Rob those damned Yankees," a strange savage voice kept screaming.

Then the fretful night was over. Belle crept about her room. From a trunk she took her dead brother Ed's guns. The same big forty-fours she had worn on the guerrilla trail. It had been two years now since she had touched them. The belt was still loaded with cartridges. She strapped it about her waist. Then dropped her hands on the gun butts. . . . How good they felt. . . .

Unbuckling the guns she rolled them, a few riding clothes, and some personal things in a blanket. Then making sure her parents didn't see her, she slipped to the barn and hid the bundle in some hay.

Belle returned from the barn and helped her mother prepare breakfast. During the meal she made trivial conversation with her parents. Cole said little. He finished before the others, then excused himself saying he would go pump water for the stock.

After helping her mother do the dishes and other household chores, Belle walked out into the backyard and found Cole squatting under a cottonwood, reading his Bible. She touched him on the shoulder. "Cole, I notice you read the Bible a lot."

He stood and looked at her. His blue eyes seemed to sadden. "Yes, I do. If the world and my life ever meet in peace, I want to preach."

"Wonderful." Belle's voice was sincere.

"Do you ever study the Bible?" Cole asked.

"Yes, a lot. Proverbs is my favorite book."

He closed the Bible. "Have you told your folks of your plans?"

"No, I decided not to. They wouldn't understand. It would just cause a scene that I don't want. You ride off in the morning and I'll meet you at the Cottonwood Springs."

Cole frowned, trying to put a rebuttal against her plans together. He liked John and Eliza Shirley, but there were other reasons. They were sure to get angry. They could cause him problems, big trouble. Belle read his thoughts. "You don't have to worry about my folks talking. They will be hurt. I'll be sorry, but I've made up my mind." She patted his cheek. "See you at the springs in the morning." Before he could answer she hurried back to the house.

Cole walked toward the barn. He didn't like the setup and he didn't understand Belle. But he was in a corner. There was no other choice. Then there was another problem. What would his men think of a woman riding with them?

John Shirley was in the barn repairing a saddle. He looked up when Cole entered. "Cole, will you hold the end of this loose string while I pull it tight?"

"Sure."

"Thanks," Shirley said and hung the saddle on a peg. "I've been intending to fix that thing for a month, but just been putting it off."

Cole cut him off. "Mr. Shirley, I think I'll saddle up and ride on my way."

Shirley said, "No hurry, son, you're welcome to stay as long as you wish."

"I know, Mr. Shirley, and I thank you very much for your kindness, but I guess I'll ride on."

CHAPTER FIVE

Belle went to bed early, sleeping soundly. Her mother called her for breakfast as usual. Belle went about the morning chores making sure not to arouse her parents' suspicions. When she was through she said she would ride over and check the mares in the back pasture again. Her father thought that was a good idea.

Cole was waiting, reading his Bible when she rode up. He didn't make much of a greeting, just closed his Bible and mounted his horse. They rode side by side for several minutes before Cole spoke. "The rest of the boys are about a mile back in those hills to the north, camped in a ravine."

"I thought they were in Dallas," Belle said.

"They were, but they rode out here day before yesterday."

"How did you know? I didn't see any of them around."

"We have ways of keeping in touch, you'll learn."

The men at the camp seemed surprised to see Belle ride in with Cole. She looked striking, dressed in men's clothes, the two big guns about her hips, mounted on a big thoroughbred sorrel gelding, the best of her father's herd. Cole swung from his saddle. "Fellows, you met Belle Shirley." He paused to place his words. "Well, she is going to ride with us."

The men looked at each other in bewilderment, then back at Cole. One of the other Younger boys laughed. "Anyway it will improve the scenery."

Belle didn't like the remark, but it broke the tension. However, she could tell by the men's expressions they resented her. It would take time, but she would prove she was as tough as they were and gain their respect.

Cole said, "Boys, mount up—we are going to ride north, got a little business up that way."

Soon they were riding, heading into the Indian Territory. Belle rode stirrup to stirrup with Cole at the head of the gang—the King and Queen. Her heart felt light, this was real life.

They followed the Texas Trail across the Indian Territory. They were in no hurry. Cole knew many people along the trail. Most were Choctaws who had fought with the Confederacy during the war. The conversations usually turned to the Yankee reconstruction depression. The Choctaws were as bitter as Cole and his gang. This pleased Belle. As they neared the confluence of the North and South Canadian rivers for the first time Belle saw the beautiful country which someday would become her home.

Belle's world was glorious, riding through the wild country and sleeping under the stars with Cole at night. Cole said nothing of his plans or their destination. Then near the Missouri line they stopped and set up a camp, and Cole called a meeting. "Boys, while we've been riding, I've been doing some thinking. A week from tomorrow is the first of the month. And a big Army payroll will arrive at Springfield. At most there won't be over thirty Feds at the post. The rest are out patrolling the countryside and don't return until weekends."

He paused, then continued. "If we hit them late in the afternoon, say around four o'clock, there will be nothing to it."

Bob Younger cut in. "Sounds good to me, but first we need to scout the place. Belle can do the job."

Belle felt both rebellious and elated. She resented being ordered around, but Cole had confidence in her scouting ability. A raid on a damned Yankee camp! Old memories flashed, excitement boiled.

Belle changed into the lady's clothes she had brought and rode into Missouri. She felt a sad feeling as she crossed the line into the old home state she had once loved. The scouting was easy. She followed the same routine she had used so successfully during the war. The soldiers at the post were glad to greet and admit a beautiful young lady. Again she was Mary Chouteau from the Cherokee Nation going to Springfield on business. A young officer was delighted to give her a tour of the post, commissary, mess and paymaster's office.

Belle recorded every detail. She spent most of the day at the post. When she left, she decided it was too late to start the return trip to the outlaw camp. And it had been a long time since she had visited Springfield. It was too great an opportunity to miss. So she rode into town and checked into a hotel, signing the register "Mary Chouteau."

The hotel was new, deluxe with a bathroom equipped with a barbershop bathtub. After the many days on the trail Belle decided to indulge in the luxury of a hot bath. She lavished herself in the tub for an hour. Clean and refreshed she ate in the dining room. Good life, she thought, but the back trails were more exciting.

After eating she went to the lobby. Several

guests, drummers, Texas cattlemen, and other travelers were sitting around swapping stories. The scene made her homesick for her happy childhood life. She took a seat in a corner and listened with the same interest she had years before. The manner of hotel lobby gossip hadn't changed. It drifted from California, to cattle drives, then settled on the main subject—a new crime, bank robbery.

Belle concentrated on the conversation, not wanting to miss the slightest detail. No one knew who was robbing the banks. The robberies were being pulled off by fast-riding, straight-shooting gangs, who just descended on a town, shooting and yelling, then looted the bank and vanished. An exciting picture formed in her mind: Cole leading his gang and her riding by his side.

During the conversation another drummer checked in. After signing the register, he turned and scanned the room, spoke to several of the guests he knew, then his eyes stopped on Belle. Her heart skipped a beat. She remembered him. He had called on her father in Carthage before the war. There was no doubt, he recognized her. He stepped toward her and smiled. "My gosh, Myra Belle Shirley, I can hardly believe my eyes."

She had to keep her poise and think fast. "Sir, I'm afraid there must be some mistake."

He studied her. Then shook his head. "I'm sorry, ma'am, for a moment I thought you were someone I knew."

Belle knew he wasn't fooled. Her mind raced, but she couldn't remember his name. It started with an H— Henry, no, that wasn't it. Harrison from St Louis, sold saddles and gear. Everything came back now. Harrison was a close friend of her father and a Southern sympathizer. He had played her game in the lobby. But would he place her with the Youngers and their gang in the upcoming robbery? She had to know.

A few minutes after Harrison went upstairs the innkeeper left the desk for the dining room. Belle got up and walked by the desk, glancing at the open register. Harrison was in room five. She turned, nodded to the other guests, then climbed the stairs as if turning in for the night.

She paused, thought, then tapped Harrison's door. The door creaked. "Come on in, young lady," Harrison smiled.

Stepping inside she pushed the door closed with her heel. "You were correct, Mr. Harrison, I'm Myra Belle Shirley." Then she leaned forward and kissed Harrison's cheek. "I'm sorry about what happened downstairs. Lord, it's good to see an old friend." She was sincere.

Harrison took Belle's hands in his. "Don't worry. I'm sure you had your reasons for denying your name. Now sit down and tell me about your family, and yourself."

Belle took the chair offered her, the only one in the room. Harrison seated himself on the bed. Just like the good ole days, Belle thought, around people she could trust.

Harrison opened the conversation. "It sure hurt to see you and your family move to Texas, but I understand. How is it down there?"

Belle talked several minutes about her family, how the new horse-ranching venture was prospering, and their establishment of a new life. Then she said, "I know you are wondering why I didn't want to be recognized." She paused and placed her words. Harrison was a smart man; she didn't want to tell a story he wouldn't believe. "I came back to see if there might be any way we could recover some of the property we were forced to abandon. Too many people would recognize Father. Since I've grown and changed I came using an assumed name."

Harrison's expression told Belle he believed her story. "Your idea is good. However, it will never work. No one who knew you will ever forget those beautiful black eyes."

His voice raised in emotion. "Missouri has turned into a living hell. Carpetbaggers are running the state. Anyone on the side of the South is open game. I'm just barely making a living. I have to kick back on my profits or be run out of business, maybe killed. Take my advice, little lady, and go back to Texas. No doubt, but what some carpetbagging Yankee has title to your father's property. Forget it."

He looked her in the eyes. "And if you are recognized you will be arrested. You're a Shirley, and that name is high on the Feds' list."

That violent revenge craving was in full flame again. Oh how sweet the upcoming robbery would be. She cleared her mind. Harrison must not suspect. "Thank you, Mr. Harrison, we have heard the same stories in Texas. I guess I should forget the matter and go home."

"Please, Myra Belle, if you stay around, it will just mean trouble."

She stood. "Thanks, I guess our dreams were foolish. Father won't be too disappointed, he held little hope. I'll get up early and head back."

Harrison opened the door. "I'll be up early too. Can we have breakfast together, Mary Chouteau?"

Belle's face flushed. Harrison smiled. "Good night, Myra Belle."

CHAPTER SIX

Belle was up early, five A.M. Harrison was waiting in the dining room. Belle ordered a heavy breakfast—eggs, sausage, and some ham sandwiches wrapped to go for lunch on the trail. They made little conversation during the meal, and when they finished Harrison handed Belle an envelope. "That's a letter to your folks. I better go now, someone might recognize you." He walked around the table and kissed her forehead. "Good luck, honey."

Belle had mixed feelings as she headed her horse into the early morning semidarkness. Harrison was such a fine person, but he was weak. Why the hell did he let the damned Yankees push him around? To leave would be better. Start a new life someplace else. Better to run than be tormented. Yes, run, but kill two or three, then run.

It was after dark when she rode into the outlaw camp. Cole was a little edgy. "I was beginning to get worried. What was the holdup?" he asked.

She gave him a detailed report, except for meeting Harrison; he might not understand. Cole didn't interrupt, just listened. "It's there for the taking. Should be easy," she finished.

Cole said, "Good job." Then he turned to the rest of the gang sprawled about camp. "Everyone gets to sleep. We're riding at three in the morning."

65

Belle slept little as she lay by Cole on a blanket. She gazed at the quarter moon. Five years before it had been the same kind of night, the night before she led Bloody Bill Anderson on her first raid. The same excitement and urge to destroy her enemy was back.

The early breakfast was strips of bacon, cold biscuits and coffee. Then Cole outlined his strategy. They would ride in pairs so as not to attract attention, then meet in a creek-bottom five miles west of Springfield and camp overnight.

Cole and Belle rode together. There was little talk, each engrossed in their own thoughts. They were the first to arrive at the designated meeting place. After their horses were cared for Belle dozed on a blanket, Cole read his Bible. By late afternoon, the rest of the gang was in camp. Cole said, "We camp here overnight, to rest us and our horses. Tomorrow is it. Now we're in enemy country, follow the same guard schedule. We don't want to get slipped-up on."

Belle admired Cole's thoroughness. Again she couldn't sleep; the early dawn was welcome. After another small breakfast and meeting, Cole detailed his plan for the robbery. The payroll would arrive at the Army post at ten. The convoy of guards bringing it would hang around until after lunch, then leave. The camp would be lazy and drowsy after eating, like "sitting ducks." The gang would hit just as soon as the convoy was a safe distance away, out of gunshot hearing. Each man was assigned a specific duty. The guards at the gate and the paymasters were to be clubbed, no shooting.

Anger built up within Belle as Cole made the assignments. She was ignored. "And me?" she snapped.

"Cool down, angel. I didn't forget you. If you rode

in there you would be recognized and the jig would be up. So you will stay in that rim of trees east of the gate and be our rear guard."

He turned to the men. "In case we get in a chase, ride straight toward where Belle is hidden."

Belle cut in. "And I'm to open fire on the pursuers, right?"

"Right. We'll be depending on you."

"Don't worry."

"All right, everything is set. After we make the hit and get clear we scatter. Then in two weeks we meet at the same place in St. Louis."

The men checked horses, guns, gear, then drifted off in pairs. At one o'clock they met in the wooded area east of the post. There was little talk. Belle felt the old tingle of revenge. They watched the armed convoy ride out. Cole checked his watch, waited thirty minutes, turned and nodded to his men.

The gang mounted and edged to the rim of brush, their faces eager, ready to strike their enemy. Belle was smiling. The gate guards were dozing, suspecting nothing. Cole held up his hand for attention. "We ride up to about twenty yards of them. Then stick the spurs to your horses. Club the guards before they can wake up. Let's go."

Led by Cole, the gang walked their horses from the brush. Belle dismounted, pulled her Winchester from her saddle, levered a cartridge into the chamber and squatted to one knee. The guards didn't notice the approaching riders. Cole raised his right hand, then swept it downward. The horses leaped forward, spurred by steel and wild rebel yells.

The gang was upon the guards. Two of the raiders leaned in their saddles and clubbed the startled men in their tracks. Belle watched in strange delight. Then the riders were lost in a cloud of dust as they entered the post. She strained her ears for a sound of battle, but there was none. In only a matter of minutes, the riders poured from the post, heading straight for her.

Belle strained her eyes for any sign of pursuit. There was none. Across the saddle in front of Cole were two heavy canvas bags. He tossed them on the ground in front of Belle. Turning in the saddle, he checked again for pursuit. There was no activity outside the post. "All right, men, scatter out. See you in a couple of weeks." The men waved and headed into the brush.

Cole dismounted and loaded the heavy bags on a pack horse. After securing the loot on the pack saddle and covering it with blankets, they rode.

Belle and Cole kept to the back trails until dark, then made camp in a draw. After caring for their horses they built a small fire. Other than giving directions of travel there had been no conversation during the ride. With some coffee brewed and salt meat crackling in a skillet Cole carried the heavy bags of loot over by the fire.

Belle moved the skillet from the fire and watched Cole open one of the bags. The contents glistened by the firelight. Gold—gold coins, hundreds of them shining and winking. She gloated, not from greed, but revenge. That was damned Yankee gold. They had taken it, taken it by force. She ran over, dipped and rattled handfuls. Cole watched emotionless, then smiled. "We hurt them, babe, biggest haul yet."

"Damned Yankees," Belle continued to mumble under her breath and gloat. Then holding a double handful of coins, she turned to Cole. "What's our plans? We can't ride all the way to St. Louis leading a pack horse, too suspicious."

Cole patted her cheek. "Always thinking. You are right. I have an idea. Will your horse work to a buggy?"

"Sure, all our horses are buggy broke."

"We might as well travel in style. In the morning take some of the Yankee gold into Springfield and buy a buggy and harness."

Belle was in town at daybreak. She bought the fanciest buggy and gear she could find. And she couldn't resist the temptation of a dress shop, leaving with a lady's dress and matching finery.

As usual Cole was reading his Bible when she returned. He folded the Bible, then surveyed the rig. "Good, nice enough," he said to himself. Then he looked at Belle. "Did you hear anything about the robbery in town?"

"Not a word."

"What I figured. The Feds will keep it quiet. They don't want the people of Missouri to know they were raided . . . embarrassing."

Cole and Belle took their time traveling to St. Louis. They posed as wealthy Texas cattle people on vacation. When they arrived in St. Louis they checked into one of the better hotels, bought new wardrobes and impressed everyone with their manners.

Money was plentiful. The sharp couple rubbed shoulders with the elite at theaters and better restaurants. Belle loved drama and still held visions of someday being an actress. Cole's interest soon waned in shows; he preferred reading, mainly his Bible. And if not reading he liked to roam the riverfront with his brothers. Belle didn't seem to mind. She loved the opera and didn't object to Cole's other interests.

But Cole's stays away from the hotel suite

became longer. Sometimes he would be gone for a week. He never told Belle where he had been. He would just put on his hat and say, "I'll be back in a day or two, got some business to look after."

This Belle didn't like. She was suspicious. Almost weekly the papers were publishing accounts of bank robberies. She was being left out of the action. When she tried to question Cole he just sulked and read his Bible.

Cole's secret visits went on for several weeks. Then late one night after a long absence he was taken by surprise. Belle had just learned something which was going to change their lifestyle. Whether she would be happy or sad would be up to Cole.

"Cole, we are going to have a baby."

He froze in disbelief.

"We are going to have a baby," Belle repeated.

The astonishment was gone, replaced by a devilish temper. "You're lying," Cole snapped.

"No, I'm not lying."

"You damned lowdown hussy. You sorry little—"

The words hung in his throat. He was looking in the muzzle of a gun in Belle's hand. "If you weren't the father of my unborn child I'd blow your damned head off. No one curses or slurs Belle Shirley. Now get your clothes and git."

Cole Younger wasn't afraid of man or beast, but this was neither. In front of him was a she-devil. The same one Bill Anderson and Jim Dancer had talked about. She stepped closer. "I said get out, you Bible-reading son of a bitch." Cole flinched. That voice—cold, keyed to a death pitch.

He didn't take time to pack, just whirled and walked from the room knowing he was lucky.

Next morning Belle packed and headed for her

parents' home in Texas, driving the same rig which had brought her and Cole Younger to St. Louis. This trip was more proof that Belle knew no fear. Most of this trip was through the Indian Territory, so wild that few men ventured into the region alone.

Two weeks later Belle arrived at her parents' home. John and Eliza Shirley were again overjoyed at their daughter's return, after five months and no word. Then the joy turned to shame when Belle told them she was pregnant. There would be rural gossip and their beloved daughter would be shunned.

But Belle saved her parents from disgrace and embarrassment, cheating the gossips of their pleasure. She visited neighbors, attended all socials, telling everyone she was the victim of a worthless husband who walked out on her when she became pregnant. The community bought the story, so instead of being buried in disgrace, she became the object of sympathy.

In the spring of 1867, exact birthdate unknown, Belle gave birth to a baby girl.

Eliza Shirley named her new granddaughter Pearl, after an aunt. The Shirleys loved baby Pearl dearly even though they hated Cole Younger. After the baby was a few months old Belle decided to return to school. Her parents were pleased and Eliza Shirley was more than willing to care for her granddaughter.

Again Belle did well in school. She studied and worked hard at the piano and drama. Seeing the plays and operas in St. Louis had motivated her even more to become an actress. Though she never mentioned to her parents her adventures on the outlaw trail the memories flashed daily. And as hard as she tried, Cole Younger wouldn't go away. She remembered the good times—riding hell-bent across the wild prairies and making love under the stars.

The daydreaming caused the restlessness to stir in Belle. She tried to fight it off. It became a nagging nightmare interfering with her studies. Her surroundings didn't help. She loathed the rural life after St. Louis. Most of their neighbors were ne'er-do-well farmers, just above poverty and jealous of the prosperous Shirleys.

One of the neighbors started a rumor (true) that the father of Belle's child was the notorious outlaw Cole Younger and that the two were never married. Belle was about to be disgraced by what she considered scum. One evening after school she rode to the gossip's home. He was standing in front of his house. Without a word she leaned from her saddle, snatched his hat, threw it in the air and shot three holes through the crown. "Now, you son of a bitch, any more talk about me and I won't take your hat off to put the hole through it."

That was the end of the gossip, but another tragedy struck the Shirley family. Preston, the oldest son, had sold his ranch and moved to Dallas, taking a job as a faro dealer in a saloon. John Shirley protested, but Preston assured his father he ran an honest game in a high-class place.

Belle and her parents were playing with baby Pearl on the front porch when a strange rider rode up. "Is this the John Shirley home?" the rider asked.

Shirley stepped off the porch. "Yes, I'm John Shirley. What can I do for you."

"I've brought you some bad news."

"What news?" Shirley asked.

"Your son, Preston, was shot and killed last night."

"Oh, my God, no!" Mrs. Shirley shouted.

"I'm sorry, folks." The rider reined his horse to leave. But Belle grabbed the bridle. "I want to know what happened. Who killed my brother?"

"A drunken gambler, Joe Lynn." The rider eyed Belle. "Uncalled for, ma'am, cold blood."

"Where is my brother's body?"

"They buried him this morning in the Dallas cemetery."

"Well, I'll be damned," Belle said. "We didn't even get the chance to give him a decent burial."

"I'm sorry, folks." The rider nodded and rode off.

John and Eliza Shirley stood, heads bowed in silence, but not Belle. She ran into the house, emerging in a few minutes dressed as a man. About her waist were the two big forty-fours.

John Shirley was aghast. "Myra Belle, my God, what are you up to!"

"I'm going after Joe Lynn, whoever the son of a bitch is."

"No, no, you can't!" her mother cried.

"I'm going. Look after Pearl." She ran to the barn and saddled a horse. Her parents were stunned as she vanished in a cloud of dust. Was that their daughter?

Belle checked into a Dallas hotel, then started a search for her brother's killer. She made a striking figure, going from saloon to saloon asking about Joe Lynn, making no bones about her mission: gun down her brother's killer. First the bartenders grinned at the young woman with the big guns on her shapely hips. Then their stares would move upward and pause on the round bosom before being locked in the grip of those deadly black eyes. The smiles froze; this woman meant business. But a woman going after a gunfighter of Joe Lynn's caliber, they shook their heads.

One bartender made the mistake of letting his thoughts become words. "Honey, I know Joe Lynn. I'm sure he would just love for a young filly like you to kill him, love him to death, you know."

She whirled, both guns popping, and several billiard balls on a nearby table flew into dust. "Now, you son of a bitch, tell Joe Lynn I'm looking for him, and not to make love."

Lynn soon heard Belle was looking for him. He also heard some exaggerated versions of her prowess with a six-shooter. Regardless of whether he believed the stories or not, Lynn didn't stay around to test Belle's skill with a gun.

Belle was disapoointed when she heard her prey had fled Dallas. He had cheated her; revenge was what she wanted. Furious, she went on a three-day drinking, cursing and hell-raising spree, racing her horse through the streets, yelling and shooting out street lights. Dallas buzzed of the young she-devil on the loose.

With her frustrations quenched, Belle sobered and took stock. Should she return home? The bright lights and action around Dallas won. The craving had to be fed. To stay she must have money. After some thinking she took a job as an entertainer in a saloon, playing the piano and dancing. The job was good tonic, fulfilling her desire to act, satisfying with good pay.

Belle's life would have been complete, except for a nagging feeling of guilt at leaving her baby. It was too strong. After two weeks Belle was home.

Joe Lynn fled, she told her parents, and she never mentioned working in a saloon. The Shirleys were happy to have their daughter, now their only living child home.

An advanced school had just started in Scyene and Belle enrolled, much to the satisfaction of her parents. (Studying and learning was a trademark Belle carried through life, always keeping a well-stocked library.)

Soon Belle became the top student in school. Her musical talent became known throughout the region. She was asked to play at most of the important social and community events. The Shirleys were proud of their daughter.

Joe Pendergrass, a young teacher at the school, became very fond of Belle, and became a frequent visitor at the Shirley home. Belle's parents encouraged the budding courtship. Belle was friendly with the young teacher, but that was all.

Belle realized that even though she was giving him no encouragement, Pendergrass was becoming serious. One evening she invited him for a walk. When they were a safe distance from the house she found a seat on a boulder. "Joe, take a good close look at me. What do you see?"

Joe blushed and stammered, "A beautiful woman."

"What I thought and was afraid of. Joe, there is much, much more. You aren't seeing the real me. Maybe I can't even see my real self." Patting the space beside her, she said, "Sit down." She paused and searched for words that wouldn't form, stared into space several minutes, then turned and kissed his cheek. "Joe, let's just be friends, good friends, that's all."

The young man was heartbroken. "I love you. I want you to be my wife," he stammered.

"No, Joe, it would be no good. It just wouldn't

work. You'll get over this. The right woman will come along."

But Pendergrass didn't give up. He continued to hang around, riding home from school with Belle daily. Belle would have run him off, but didn't want to hurt and embarrass her parents. To her he became a pest that she didn't know how to handle.

One afternoon on her way home, with the young teacher riding by her side, Belle saw several riders top a rise in front of them. As they approached her heart jumped; the one in the lead, that carefree easy sway in the saddle, was Cole Younger.

Cole was as surprised as Belle. He jerked his horse to a halt. They were eye to eye. "Why, hello, Mr. Younger."

Cole just sat and stared. The other riders milled around. "I said hello. Remember me?" One of the riders chuckled. Cole still didn't speak. "Cat got your tongue?" Belle smirked. That did it. Cole sprang from his saddle and in the same motion swept Belle into his arms.

He tried to force his lips to hers. Instead he got both of her fists in his eyes. He loosened his hold and reeled backward, blinking. "What the hell!" he shouted. Another blow smacked hard on his mouth, a spray of blood spewing to one side.

Before Cole could recover from the assault Belle jumped on her horse, spurs digging. Sometime during the fracas Pendergrass laid the whip to his horse and fled. He had seen and heard enough.

Belle said nothing to her parents about the incident. After dinner she dressed in her best lady's clothes, as Cole Younger would be calling. This was not a hunch—she knew the man. And she had to admit she wanted him to call. Hitting him was sweet revenge, but the old fire was blazing.

As usual after dinner Belle and her parents sat on the front porch playing with baby Pearl. Belle heard fast-approaching horses. She was correct. Cole was calling. She picked up Pearl and walked to the yard gate as the riders pulled up. "Good evening, Mr. Younger. You and the other boys tie up and come in," Belle said.

John Shirley fought back his dislike for Cole Younger, but shook his hand. Cole was the father of his granddaughter. "Good evening, Mr. Shirley, good to see you again." Younger's voice carried a sincere tone. Then he turned to one of his men. "Come here, Jim."

A slender young man stepped beside Cole. "Remember him, Judge?"

Shirley studied the young man's face. "My God, son, you're a grown man now, but I remember you, our neighbor boy in Missouri, Jim Reed." He grabbed Reed's shoulders. "Son of a gun, but it is good to see you. Belle, you and Eliza come here."

Belle and her mother remembered Jim Reed and embraced him. After the meeting all except Belle and Cole went into the house. They sat in the porch swing, Belle cradling Pearl in her arms. The conversation was whispered and sincere. Cole apologized, asked forgiveness and expressed his love for Belle. He was ready to settle down. The last big bank robbery had netted thousands of dollars. They could buy a ranch and raise their daughter.

Belle accepted Cole's apology and said she loved him. However, she dictated the terms of their new arrangement. She wouldn't be hurt again. If either tired of their deal, they would shoot square, no feuding and fighting.

In a few days Cole and Belle bought a tract of

nearby land, putting the title in Belle's name. Then they went about building a small house and barns, and making other improvements. Soon they had a thriving little thoroughbred horse ranch stocked with blooded animals. Where all the fine horses came from caused some raised eyebrows.

When not working their ranch Cole and Belle visited neighbors and attended social affairs. Both seemed to enjoy their new life. Cole always found time during each day to read the Bible. He searched for passages which justified his robbing the rich.

A firm believer in "An eye for an eye and a tooth for a tooth," Cole was quick to expound his philosophies of life when an audience was available.

While Cole was busy with the Bible, Belle practiced the piano and read classic literature, dramas being her favorites. But the quiet lifestyle was boring to both. They were excitement people, with daring in their veins. One morning Cole looked up from his breakfast plate. "Belle, it's no use. I've got to ride."

Belle nodded. "I understand. Good luck." Cole kissed Belle and Pearl, laid a big roll of bills on the table, and rode.

CHAPTER SEVEN

With Cole Younger out of her life, Belle went about planning her own future. It wouldn't be at Scyene on a horse ranch. There was more to life. She sold off the horses and headed to Dallas, leaving Pearl with her parents.

In Dallas she went back to entertaining in the saloons. Soon her fame spread. All the better places bid for her act: playing the piano, singing, and cracking jokes. Belle's shows were the nearest thing to class in the wild cowtown. Life was beautiful, with excitement, money, and no lack of male companionship of the higher social level. Many stood in line trying to gain favor with the dark-haired beauty.

While working as an entertainer Belle learned another profession, gambling. When not putting on her act she spent most of her spare time hanging around the gaming tables, observing and studying. Poker in particular fascinated her. It was a game of skill—brains, money and guts. Her game. Being blessed with an abundance of all three, she could win, win big. She studied and prepared. Poker was a game of life: the strong and smart survived, the weak perished.

Belle spent hours in her hotel room practicing dealing and figuring odds of the draw. Soon her quick mind and nimble musician's fingers mastered the game. But she didn't hurry. She wanted to be

79

sure the odds were hers before hitting the tables.

One night while going through her act she kept an eye on a high-stakes game. The gamblers were rich cattlemen, bankers and a professional gambler. When her last act of the evening was over she took a seat near the big game. Then her chance came. One of the cattlemen excused himself, complaining of not feeling well.

When the man left, Belle moved over to the table. "Gentlemen, may I take the vacant chair?"

The gamblers looked up from their cards in astonishment. A woman wanting to sit in a high-stakes game—must be another of the entertainer's jokes. They laughed. Belle boiled, but fought back her temper. "What do you say, gentlemen?"

One of the men laughed. "She might sweeten up the pot." The others ha-hawed. Belle thought, *Just let me in, I'll sweeten your damned pot alright, I'll break your ass*. The professional gambler said, "Suits me, honey, five thousand dollars change in, table stakes, dealer's choice."

Belle pulled a large roll of bills from someplace under her fluffy dancer's skirt and pitched it on the table. "Ten thousand. Want to count it, gentlemen?"

The men's stares bounced back and forth from the roll of bills, to each other, then to Belle, surprised. Finally the gambler said, "No, just play it."

Belle lost a few hundred feeling her way and studying the players. Some were playing it close, one loudmouthed rancher was a bluffer, the gambler was both skilled and crooked. She watched his middle finger sneak a King off the bottom to fill a straight. When the gambler dealt she folded, even though she had Aces wired. He was trying to set her up.

Then it was her deal. She fumbled with the cards, pretending to be awkward, not wanting to arouse suspicion. Whacking the deck on the table she asked, "Cuts, burns or bruises, gentlemen?"

The loudmouth roared. "Hell no, anyone as pretty as you couldn't be crooked. Deal, but what's your game?"

"The name of the game is stud, five-card." She called out the cards as she dealt around the table. By the fourth card turn all the players folded except Belle, loudmouth and the gambler. Loudmouth held three Queens showing. They studied each other's hands, comparing and thinking. The gambler had a ten-high straight working. Belle studied her two sevens showing; the third one was in the hole. The gambler raised a thousand. Loudmouth called and tried a bluff with a two-thousand raise, making it three thousand up to Belle. Her brow wrinkled. This was it. She had the gambler beat, unless he hit his straight, but three sevens wouldn't beat three Queens. "Come on. Get on or off," Loudmouth touted.

Belle still fretted. "Did you come to play or pray?" Loudmouth chuckled. Finally Belle picked up her money, counted, then hesitated. "In or out?" Loudmouth asked again.

He was right. She had come to gamble. The gambler showed no emotion until Belle tossed her money in the pot. Then he gave her a confused stare, but called. Belle started the deal. Loudmouth drew the gambler's nine. The gambler landed an Ace, grinned and folded. Belle had to have the fourth seven. She flipped her card. The seven came. Loudmouth was now wild-eyed with eagerness and confidence. No doubt the nine had paired his hole card, giving him a full house, Queens over nines, then again he could have that fourth Queen in the hole. "How much in your stack, baby doll?"

"Sixty-five hundred," Belle replied.

He pitched a wad of money in the pot. "Let's go to tap city."

Belle didn't hesitate. She pitched in her bundle.

"Read 'em and weep, baby," Loudmouth roared, whipping over his hole card. "Queens full of nines."

"Sorry, big hoss," Belle smiled, "four sevens."

"I'll be a son of a bitch, damned beginner's luck!" Loudmouth cursed.

Belle raked in the big pot, not quite all luck. The seven had been on the bottom of the deck with Loudmouth's Queen, the next card.

Soon Belle's reputation spread as a gambler. She was hired as a dealer in some of the best saloons in Dallas. Men lined up "to buck the lady dealer." Most left several dollars poorer and a lot wiser.

Belle loved gambling. Not only did she find it exciting, satisfying and profitable, but it also gave her the feeling of superiority over men. With a strange savage indifference she parted men from their money, smiling as her victims sweated and squirmed.

Dallas buzzed about the flashy dealer, her dress getting as much talk as her gambling skills. Belle hired a dressmaker and designed her own clothes. Her outfits were many and varied, all designed to show off her shapely figure. But the accessories and trim drew the most attention. A man's soft white Stetson was always cocked over the jet-black eyes, fancy hand-tooled boots encased the dainty feet and about the shapely hips were strapped a pair of silver-plated pearl-handled forty-fours. Sometimes she appeared in tailored buckskins.

Men lusted after the frontier beauty, showering her with gifts. However, it was drawing the scorn of the elite Dallas female population that gave her the most fulfillment. She flaunted and strutted in their midst at every opportunity. *The jealous bitches,* she thought, *I'm what they want to be.*

Life was beautiful for Belle. Then one night an incident gave her life another drastic twist. The gambling house was jammed, cowboys, trail drovers, gamblers, dudes and gunfighters whooping it up, celebrating someone's birthday. Painted girls moved through the crowd giggling, kissing and adding to the enjoyment. Everyone was in a good mood. Belle was dealing a high-stake faro game.

In full concentration on her game, she didn't notice a young man standing at the rear of the crowd watching her deal, then elbow his way to her table. "This is a crooked game," he sneered.

The crowd hushed. Men glanced at each other. Was the fancy lady gambler as good with a gun and as tough as she acted? The question was on their faces. They got a quick answer. Magically there was a mean short forty-four in her right hand pointed at the young stranger's head. He was beat. One move and he was dead. Those piercing eyes behind the cocked gun told the story. Smoke drifted between the two. The young man blew it away, then laughed. "Myra Belle Shirley, you wouldn't really shoot a good ole Missouri boy, would you?"

"Well, I'll be damned, Jim Reed. What are you doing here?"

"Come to see you. Hoped you would remember me, from the time we met at your folks' a while back."

Belle ran around the table and embraced Reed. The crowd relaxed. "All right, the game is closed for tonight. I'm going to do a little celebration with an old friend."

After a few drinks Belle took Reed to her hotel room. "Jim, what brings you to Dallas?" she asked.

"Cole sent me to get you."

"Cole sent you to get me. That's a big joke. Where is he? And what does he want?"

"We're camped on your farm. I have no idea what he wants to talk with you about."

Belle laughed. "Excuse me, Jim. I'm not laughing at you, but this is so damned funny. The wandering husband returns. And the wife is supposed to go a-running. Why in the hell didn't he come?"

"Belle, Cole couldn't come. I thought you knew. He and most of the gang have big rewards on their heads."

"That's their problem." Belle's eyes were sparkling. She had other things on her mind. Jim Reed was a handsome young man—tough, exciting. A whirlwind romance followed. For the next week Belle escorted her new lover around Dallas. Then she did a strange thing; she rode with Reed out to the farm where Cole and his gang were camped. And as if Jim Reed had never existed she embraced Cole in a passionate greeting.

Cole said, "Belle, let's take a walk. We need to talk." When out of earshot of the others he said, "First, I'm sorry we ever became involved. It's all over now."

Belle cut in. "Cole, I'm so glad you feel that way. Because I'm in love with Jim Reed and we're going to get married."

Cole was taken by surprise. He fumbled for words, finally stammering, "Congratulations, Jim Reed is a good boy." Then regained his composure. Belle marry Jim Reed? She must be playing a game, bluffing. He would call her bluff. "Belle, that new man riding with us is John 'Preacher' Fischer, ordained Baptist minister. He decided collections were too light and joined us."

Belle read Cole's mind. She called his bluff. "Great, a real preacher. So, why not, Jim and I will be married right here and now."

With Preacher Fischer doing the honors and Cole and the other outlaws as witnesses, Myra Belle Shirley and Jim Reed became man and wife. The first to congratulate the newlyweds and kiss the bride was Cole Younger.

The new bride and groom spent the night in camp, then next morning rode to Belle's parents' home. The Shirleys were delighted with their daughter's new husband. They were sure she had made a wise choice. Reed was a clean-cut good Missouri boy. They had no idea their new son-in-law was as much of an outlaw as Cole Younger.

The Shirleys were even more delighted when Jim and Belle announced they were moving back to Missouri to make their home. As a wedding gift they gave the couple a blooded stallion and two fine mares.

Bidding the Shirleys goodbye, the Reeds took baby Pearl and headed for Missouri. What had started as a lark, Belle now saw as a new life. They had money. She envisioned regaining the old Shirley social and financial status in Missouri. Jim was the type of man she needed. He was tough, an outlaw, but not wanted like Cole Younger. And most of all he said little, letting her do the managing. This she liked most.

Belle and Jim followed the Texas Trail across the Indian Territory. They were in no hurry. The trip was their honeymoon. At North Town, they left the

Texas Trail and traveled several miles east to a great bend in the Canadian River, the home of the Starrs. Both knew several members of the large Cherokee family.

The reputation of the Starr clan was well known throughout the Indian Territory and bordering states. They were many in numbers, feared and merciless fighters. The leader was Tom Starr, who had eight sons, Sam, Cooper, Moxie, William, Ellis, Jack and Washington, and two daughters, Nettie and Sophia, along with countless other relatives.

Fanatic advocates of the Southern cause, the Starrs kept fighting after the Confederacy surrendered. They continued to wage war against the northern division of the Cherokee Nation led by the Ross faction. Several pitched battles were fought between the two groups. To stop the fighting and bring peace to the Cherokees, the Cherokee Council signed a separate treaty with the Starrs, giving them a large sum of money, hundreds of head of livestock and a huge tract of land on the Canadian, in the southwest corner of the Cherokee Nation.

After a good long rest Belle and Jim continued to Missouri. They bought a large farm near Jim's parents' at Rich Hill. The Reeds were delighted that their son was settling down. He had done well; Belle was a beautiful, educated, cultured young lady from the fine Shirley stock.

Belle and Jim entered their farming venture with a reckless vigor, planting crops, clearing land, buying and selling livestock. They were accepted by the community. Belle was in demand to play and sing for socials and churches.

The young couple's hard work soon brought prosperity and more respect. It seemed everything they touched turned to gold. But what the friends and neighbors didn't know was that much of the financial gain was not from hard work.

Occasionally Belle and Jim would leave baby Pearl with Jim's parents and be gone a few days, explaining they took camping trips, just to get away. The camping trips were joining the Younger and James boys on bank-robbing forays. Belle and Jim Reed took part in at least two bank robberies, the Liberty and the Richmond. Belle cased the banks, then hid at the edge of town while the gang pulled the stickups.

The Richmond robbery was one of the wildest ever pulled off. Not only was the bank looted by the gang, but several prisoners were freed from the town's jail. The prisoners were being held on various charges by carpetbaggers. There was a savage gunfight. The town's mayor and his son were killed. The Youngers and Jameses were recognized during the raid, but not Jim Reed. However, it was reported that a young man named Jim White was riding with the gang. Reed used White as an alias. Rewards were offered for the gang, including White.

After several months in Missouri, Belle became pregnant again. This time was different; Belle and Jim were both thrilled. The trips stopped. They stayed close to home. It looked as if the pair had quit their wild ways. They were prosperous and the coming child gave them a different look at life.

Life was beautiful for the Reeds. Then one evening Cole Younger rode in. "Belle, you are in no condition to ride," he said. "But, Jim, we need your help on a job."

Jim looked at Belle. She read the excitement in his eyes. "It's up to you, Jim. I don't mind."

"What kind of a job, Cole?" Jim asked.

"The biggest one yet. Frank James has found a bank over in Kentucky just busting with Yankee gold."

"When do we leave?" Jim was excited.

"Now."

In a few minutes Jim was packed. A week later the bank at Russelville, Kentucky, was looted. Several days after the stickup Jim returned home. Riding with him was Preacher Fischer. Belle could tell the men were worried. "How did it go?" she asked.

"Everything went according to plan," Jim answered. "But a whole army of bounty hunters and detectives are hunting the gang. Big rewards posted all over."

Belle consoled them. "Don't worry. They don't know your identity. You and Preacher would be the last two ever suspected."

She was correct; no one suspected the two as outlaws. Preacher stayed with Belle and Jim and started preaching around at nearby churches. One evening the three were talking in the living room when their conversation was interrupted by a knock on the door. Jim and Preacher grabbed their guns, stationing themselves to crossfire the door in case it was the law. Belle opened the door. It was a neighbor boy named Jackson. He ran inside. "What's wrong?" Belle asked.

The excited boy glanced about, then said to Jim, "Mr. Reed, I have bad news. One of the Shannons bushwhacked your brother Scott." Then the boy looked at Fischer. "Preacher, he thought he was getting you."

"Thank you, son," Jim said and handed the boy a gold piece. "Now you better get going."

When the boy was out the door, Jim turned to

Belle. "I may be gone a day, or a week. When I get back have me a good horse packed and ready to ride."

Belle's mind spun back to her brothers' murders. She knew the feeling, the desire for revenge. "Go, Jim, it's your honor to avenge your brother. Everything will be ready."

Jim and Preacher saddled and rode into the night. Before daylight they were back. Not one horse was packed and waiting, but two and a pack horse. "I don't need all those horses."

"I'm riding with you, Jim."

"Not in your condition, and what about Pearl?"

Belle's eyes flashed. "I'm taking Pearl with us."

Jim knew Belle. "All right, let's go." He turned to Fischer. "You going with us, Preacher?"

"No, I'm sticking around. Someone will have to preach the funerals of those two Shannons we shot."

Jim and Belle rode fast, Jim holding Pearl in front of him. They headed for the Indian Territory and the Starrs' stronghold on the Canadian.

After a few days' rest at the Starrs', Belle asked Jim, "Where do we go from here?"

"California," he replied.

Belle was thrilled, as she had heard much of the West Coast. And the thought of the long trip was appealing even in her condition. She had been penned up too long. Then she wondered why Jim had decided on California.

Rather than make the long trip on horses, they bought a buckboard from the Starrs. Not being in a hurry, Jim and Belle spent several weeks on the trail. It was a vacation-like trip. When they arrived, Belle soon discovered why Jim had picked California.

There was none other to meet them than the

James and Younger boys. After the Kentucky robbery the gang had split. Most drifted to California, all traveling by land except Jesse James. He went to New York and caught a boat around the Horn.

Soon after their arrival Belle gave birth to a son. The baby boy was named Eddie after one of Jim's uncles. With their new son the Reeds tried family life again. With plenty of money and hundreds of miles from the Missouri laws they had no worries, and soon gained some respectability as good citizens.

The Jameses and the Youngers were also making an effort at going straight. But a quiet life was beyond their scope. They had lived too long by their wits and guns. There was always that nagging yearning for excitement.

Then for no apparent reason other than excitement the Youngers and the Jameses held up a stagecoach near San Diego. After the holdup the gang headed back east, leaving Jim and Belle.

Belle was glad the gang was gone, and hoped they were out of her life forever. She was making a sincere effort to forget the wild life and raise her children. She watched Jim grow more restless each day, longing for his old friends and the wild freedom. He wanted to ride. Deep inside so did she. But now it was different; she had two children and loved them dearly.

Jim tried too; he took several jobs trying to settle down, but the longing was still there even months after the rest of the gang left. One day Belle said, "We must make up our minds. If we are going to stay here we have got to start a ranch or do something worthwhile. We can't go on like this. We are both going mad."

Jim replied. "Let's face it, Belle, California isn't

for us. The climate, the people are wonderful. But I'm homesick."

The next day they loaded their belongings in a wagon and headed east. For a few months Belle and Jim wandered around the Arizona and New Mexico Territories before ending up at their friends the Starrs' in the Indian Territory. Belle loved the wild primitive life in the Territory. It was a place of freedom with no interference from the law. Jim helped the Starrs work cattle, hunt and helped Belle with the children. But he was still lonesome for the Youngers and the owlhoot trails. One morning he kissed Belle and the children and rôde.

Belle and the children stayed with the Starrs a few more weeks, then headed for her parents' in Texas. Again the Shirleys welcomed their daughter and their grandchildren. But John Shirley had had enough. He laid down the law to Belle. She and the children could stay as long as they wished, "but none of her outlaw male companions could come around." The Texas laws were hounding him, accusing him of harboring criminals.

Soon after Belle returned home, Jim Reed rode in. Shirley didn't suspect Reed of being an outlaw and welcomed him with open arms. Belle had explained she and Jim had just had a small fuss.

Jim had just helped the Youngers and James boys pull off a big bank robbery in Iowa. He was loaded with loot. Telling Shirley they had saved the money in California, Belle and Jim bought another small ranch.

Things went smoothly for awhile. No one in the area even suspected the boyish-looking Reed of being a tough outlaw and gunman. Then one day John Shirley made a business trip to Dallas. A wanted poster caught his attention. It read, "Jim

White Wanted for Bank Robbery."

Shirley studied the poster in disbelief. The picture, the description ... the outlaw wasn't Jim White, but his son-in-law, Jim Reed.

John Shirley was furious. He rode straight and hard to Belle and Jim's home. And in no uncertain terms told them to stay away from his home. Jim became uneasy. He wasn't afraid of Shirley talking, but if his father-in-law had recognized the poster no doubt others would. He wasn't about to stay around and wait for what he knew was certain. He saddled and headed for the Indian Territory.

CHAPTER EIGHT

Belle grew restless. After a few weeks she left her children with her parents and followed Jim to the Starrs' headquarters. Soon after Belle's arrival she and Jim made friends with a drifter, Dan Evans. Evans told them he knew a robbery that could be pulled off which would be more lucrative than a bank and a lot less dangerous.

Of course Belle and Jim were all ears. So on a cold November night the three rode into the Creek Nation, a few miles west of Eufaula, to the home of Walt Grayson, a wealthy old Creek Indian. Belle was dressed as a boy and under the pretense of being lost gained entry to the Grayson home. Jim and Evans followed with drawn guns demanding Grayson's money. The old man refused to tell them where it was hidden.

The three threatened the old man, but still he wouldn't talk. Then they looped a rope around his neck, saying they would hang him. He still refused to tell where his money was hidden. But Grayson's wife, fearing for her husband's life, brought the money from its hiding place in a cellar beneath the house.

Evans was right; it was a big haul, $40,000 in gold plus several thousands more in worthless Confederate currency.

After the robbery the three split up. Belle headed back to Texas with her saddlebags bulging. She visited awhile with her parents and children, then took off for Dallas looking for bright lights and action.

Dallas was booming in 1872-1873. Two railroads, the Houston Central and the Texas Pacific, had built through the town. The city boomed from about 1,500 to 4,000 almost overnight. Like most Western boomtowns, the population outgrew law and order. Gambling and vice ran wide-open with little interference. All of which was to Belle's liking.

She hit Dallas like a female tornado. Now a mature beauty, Belle rented the best suite in the Planters Hotel. To go with the lavish lodgings she bought a wardrobe the likes of which the West had never seen. Even the wild side of Dallas was startled and awed at some of Belle's daring, colorful outfits, all designed to show off her figure.

Of her many outfits Belle's favorite was a tailored doeskin shirt with matching vest, under which was a white silk blouse trimmed with rattlesnake rattlers and her trademark, the man's white Stetson with an ostrich plume stuck in the band. The fancy hand-tooled boots and silverplated six-shooters about her waist completed Belle's dress and caught every eye in Dallas.

In this unusual feminine attire Belle plunged into Dallas' social and business life. When she swaggered about the streets or through the doors of an establishment everything stopped; bartenders stopped pouring drinks, bankers quit counting, and others froze in astonishment. Belle didn't disappoint her audience. She gave them their money's worth, twisting and strutting. Acting was her love.

At night Belle was a regular in the high-stake

poker games around town, but not as a dealer now. She had money and was usually a big winner. After a game it was her custom to shout, "Everyone belly up to the bar and have a drink with a real woman." She was delighted by the startled expression of strangers in the house.

However, she didn't spend all her time gambling and playing. She built a big livery stable behind her hotel, stocked it with fine horses and hired the best hostler in Dallas. The stable was a fraud. Belle's real business was dealing in stolen horses. Business was good. Soon the stable gained the reputation of being among the best in the entire Southwest.

Belle's Stable was full-service, supplying all cartage needs, renting, buying, selling, trading fine horses for every need.

Now and then out of boredon Belle would fall into a devilish mood, then dash through town on a horse, shooting and yelling. These and other wild capers soon made her the toast of the town's dandies and wild bunch. But to the rest of the population, she was everything from a crazy bitch to a novelty.

It became common knowledge around town that she had ridden with several outlaws. And from these rumors she acquired the title "Outlaw Queen."

Belle selected her male companions. They had to meet certain social, financial and political standards. But from time to time she entertained other male visitors. Jim Reed would slip into town using the alias Bill Jones.

Then one day in 1875 another man called at the hotel. She answered the knock and there stood Cole Younger. Heart jumping, she pulled him inside her room. After all those years, she was still undecided whether she loved or hated him. Either way she respected Cole Younger. He was a man among men.

Going under the name of Jack Rogers, Cole didn't call on Belle to renew their old love. He considered her Jim Reed's wife and Jim was his friend. He was calling on business. He respected Belle's intelligence as much as she did his. After an affectionate greeting he stated his business. "Belle, I need your help to pull off a big job."

The old excitement boiled. "What kind of a job?"

"The stage that runs between San Antonio and Austin."

Belle laughed. "Since when would Cole Younger need help to stick up a stage?"

"Let me explain. One day each month the stage carries a huge sum of money. I need to know the day and the timetable."

Belle was all business now. "And if you get the information, do I get a full share?"

"Right."

"Then where and when do we meet?"

"Out on the farm that belongs to you and Jim, near Scyene."

"Consider it done." Belle smiled.

CHAPTER NINE

Early next morning Belle rode out of Dallas to Austin. She caught the stage for San Antonio, where she spent two days inquiring around town about property that might be for sale. This gave her an opportunity to study the stage operations without arousing suspicion. Try as she might, she couldn't pick up any information on the money shipment. She was about ready to admit defeat when she noticed that several businesses, the bank, and the stage office all had a certain day circled on their calendars. Then checking the timetable, she learned the stage left an hour early on that date. She laughed. "Simple, that was it." Real accomodating bunch, marking the date.

Belle rode to Scyene. Waiting was her husband Jim, Cole, and three strangers. The strangers were introduced as Cal Carter, J.H. Dickens, and his wife Mary.

According to Belle's information, the gang would have ten days before the stage which would be carrying the money arrived. For fear they might be detected if they stayed near Scyene, the gang rode to San Marcos and made camp. While waiting, Jim Reed probably unknowingly signed his own death warrant.

A man named Jack Woodfork owned a small

ranch near the gang's camp. He visited the camp several times and became friendly with the outlaws who were posing as traveling horse traders. Woodfork became especially friendly with Belle, who did nothing to discourage his attentions.

One evening while the rancher was visiting the camp Jim Reed hit him up for a horse trade. Woodfork had a big sorrel gelding which Jim liked. The two talked trade and bantered back and forth for an hour or so. Finally Woodfork said, "I'll usually trade anything I have, but I don't really care to trade this horse, he's a good one."

Jim liked the horse and didn't want to give up. "Yes, he is a fine horse. Tell you what I'll do. I'll give you my horse and fifty dollars to boot for him."

Woodfork shook his head. "That's a fair offer, but don't believe I'll trade." Then he thought a minute, winked at Jim and laughed. "On second thought, I might just consider your offer if you will throw in your wife."

Everyone laughed, including Belle. Jim laughed louder than the rest. "I'll just take you up on that offer. I'd rather have a good horse any day as a woman."

There was more laughter, but this time Belle didn't laugh. A man was belittling her. Jim may have been joking, but she didn't like it. She fought back her anger. "Go ahead, Jim, throw me in on the deal." Her voice was cold. "You heard me, Jim, take him up on the deal. Trade me for a horse. At last I seem to have reached the top value of being worth a good horse." She was laughing now, a strange gleam in her eyes.

Woodfork, seeing he had pushed his joke too far, said, "No, the deal is off."

Belle cut in. "No, the trade isn't off. A deal is a

deal. Jim traded me for a horse fair and square, and I'm ready to change pastures."

Cold Younger, knowing Belle's temper and not wanting trouble in the ranks, said, "We've had a good laugh, now let's forget the whole thing."

"Stay out of this, Cole. This deal is going through," Belle snapped.

"Yeaup, when I make a deal it stands," Jim Reed said.

Woodfork knew he had worked himself into a tight spot. He took Jim's fifty dollars and traded horses and started riding toward home. He hadn't traveled more than fifty yards when Belle jumped on her horse and shouted, "Hey wait up, remember you traded for me." Woodfork kicked his horse into a run, and Belle gave chase.

It was late afternoon of the next day before Belle returned. She taunted Jim. "Trade me again, I like those new pastures. Maybe you can get a team of mules for next time."

Jim didn't reply, which further angered Belle. The next few days in camp neither spoke to the other.

On April 6, 1874, Cole, Jim, Carter and Dickens robbed the San Antonio Stage. It was a big haul of several thousand dollars. The robbery went smoothly but the law was soon hot on the trail of the gang. Cole Younger and Jim Reed were recognized by the stage driver. Big rewards were posted. The Texas lawmen were determined to break up the Younger, James and Reed gang, or at least chase them out of Texas.

The outlaws split up. Belle took Mrs. Dickens and headed to Dallas. The women hadn't traveled far when Belle discovered they were being followed by lawmen. She had no fear. Cole had agreed to hide her share of the loot on her farm near Scyene. And no one had seen her and Mrs. Dickens during the robbery. So instead of trying to shake the lawmen, she intentionally slowed the pace.

As Belle had expected, a posse led by U.S. Marshal Major Purnell overtook her and Mrs. Dickens, placing them under arrest. The next day Dickens was picked up. The three were taken before a United States Commissioner for arraignment. But due to lack of evidence all three were released.

Cole and Reed rode hard and fast toward their friends, the Starrs, in the Indian Territory, with a posse of U.S. Marshals in hot pursuit. Even with all their back-trail knowledge and cunning the outlaws couldn't evade the marshals. The lawmen tracked Jim and Cole to Tom Starr's place.

The lawmen demanded the outlaws surrender, and were met by a small army of the Starr clan armed to the teeth. Old Tom Starr laughed in the marshals' faces, citing that he and his friends were only responsible to the Cherokee laws, and that the posse had a choice of leaving or being shot.

The marshals, seeing they were outgunned and that Tom Starr meant business, tried to reason. But what the lawmen didn't know was that Starr was more of an outlaw and meaner than Reed and Younger. Also, he carried an insane hate for any type of United States authority. Instead of listening to the lawmen's talk, Starr again ordered the posse to leave, to get off his property. To show he meant business he started shooting over their heads. The marshals got the message and headed back to Texas empty-handed, but more determined than ever to catch the outlaws.

After the fruitless chase into the Indian Territory, Marshal Purnell paid Belle a visit in Dallas.

With the marshal at the meeting was a small-time outlaw, John Morris. Morris had been arrested by Purnell for robbery a few weeks before, but had been released for lack of evidence.

After the meeting, Morris somehow found Jim Reed. Morris told Reed he was also wanted and the two started riding together. They moved back and forth between Texas and the Indian Territory. During this time Morris was gaining Reed's confidence. One day they stopped at a farmer's place near Paris, Texas to eat and to feed their horses. Not wanting to raise the suspicions of the farmer and his family, Reed and Morris left their guns on their saddles. During the meal Morris pretended to be sick, excused himself and went outside. When he returned he had a gun and demanded Reed to surrender, saying he was a deputy. Jim Reed wasn't about to give up without a fight. He dived under the table at Morris' legs. The two went down in a tangle. Several shots were fired as the two outlaws struggled for the gun. One of the bullets hit Jim Reed in the head, killing him instantly.

Morris tied Reed's body on his horse and carried it to Paris, where he tried to collect the reward. However, he hit a snag. A wire was sent to Belle, in Dallas, asking her to come and make indentification. She refused, then spread a story which made her a heroine in the eyes of the frontier badmen. She said she was heartbroken about the murder of her beloved Jim, but she would be damned if she would identify his body so a lowdown bounty hunter could collect the reward.

However, some others who knew Jim Reed made the identification. Morris collected the reward, and Jim Reed, father of Belle's son, was buried in a potters field at McKinney, Texas, August 10, 1874.

Belle wrote a letter to Jim's parents in Missouri swearing vengeance against his killer, but Morris lived to die of old age.

Now a legitimate widow, Belle went into mourning by moving Sheriff James F. Barkley into her hotel suite a week after Jim Reed's funeral. Now the "Bandit Queen" had the law and the outlaws in her corral.

With the sheriff for a partner Belle's livery stable soon doubled in size. Stolen horses were bought and sold openly. With things going well, Belle brought her daughter Pearl to Dallas. If nothing else, Belle loved her children and had big plans for her daughter. Pearl was to be the lady that Belle had so dreamed of being, but had been denied.

Pearl was enrolled in an exclusive school for girls, to study music and drama.

Then another tragedy struck Belle's life. Her father, John Shirley, died. Belle loved and respected her father more than anyone in the world. To her he was the finest person who ever lived. His life had been a chain of sorrows, tragedies, mental anguish and financial reverses—the war, both of his sons murdered, and his beloved daughter called the "Bandit Queen." Any one of these heartbreaks would have felled a lesser man.

Trouble followed trouble. A few weeks after John Shirley's death, Eliza Shirley followed her husband in death.

Her mother's death left Belle to care for her son Eddie as well as her daughter. Jim Reed's parents had been writing Belle regularly, wishing to see their grandson. With all her other interests Belle tried but couldn't find time to look after both of her children. So she decided to take Eddie to his grandparents in Missouri.

Belle took Eddie by train to his grandparents at Rich Hill, Missouri, and visited several days before returning to Dallas. And to her horror when she returned she found the school had placed Pearl in a hospital. The doctors told Belle the strain of school and living away from home was too much for the child, prescribing a long rest. Belle wrote to some relatives in Conway, Arkansas, and got permission to bring her daughter there for a long rest. She didn't hesitate taking Pearl to Arkansas and stayed until her daughter was on the road to recovery.

With her children in good hands Belle returned to Dallas and expanded her business ventures. It soon became known around Dallas that if some money was slipped to Belle most crimes were forgotten. She had the sheriff and the judge in her pocket.

But with all of her business and social interests life became boring to the Bandit Queen. To break the monotony and just for the pure hell of it, now and then Belle would shoot under some tenderfoot's feet, or pull some other caper to excite the local citizens. One day, however, she carried one of her stunts too far. Emma Wilson, a faro dealer and dancer at a saloon, became an admirer and close friend of Belle. Frequently the two took rides through the countryside. One day while riding they stopped at a country crossroads store. The store owner was a German who spoke little English. After the two women bought some candy Belle asked the German if he was a "damned Yankee." Whether the man misunderstood or not, he answered "yes."

Belle shouted, "I hate dammed Yankees!" Then she pulled her gun and started shooting up the place. She took dead aim on a coal-oil lamp which exploded and started a fire. In a few minutes the store burned to the ground.

The poor burned-out storeowner tried to make a complaint to the authorities, but was laughed at. No one believed his story. But a short time after the incident, Emma got drunk and told a U.S. marshal who hated Belle and had been trying to get something on her for a long time. The marshal visited the German and persuaded him to file arson charges against Belle.

The arrest was a big joke to Belle, but being betrayed by a woman wasn't. She posted bond and went looking for Emma and cornered her eating in a fashionable restaurant. The unfortunate girl tried to explain that she was drunk and was cornered into talking by the marshal. There were no excuses for squealing to the law, on a friend, in Belle's code. Poor Emma's pleas for mercy fell on deaf ears. To the astonishment of the other customers, Belle drew a gun and made Emma disrobe. Then she forced the frightened girl to dance on a table top. Afterwards she threw the terrified, naked girl out of the front door into a busy street.

The incident and Belle's upcoming trial became the talk of Dallas. The Bandit Queen loved the publicity. She wasn't worried about the outcome of the trial. The judge was her man. On the night before the trial she made the rounds of the bars, adoring all the attention she drew. In one of the saloons she met a wealthy cattleman, who made eyes and flashed a big roll of money. Of course Belle was interested. She told the gentleman she was a poor, broke, innocent girl, being dragged into court on trumped-up charges, and was prison-bound.

The cattleman's heart melted. Some time during the night in a hotel room he gave Belle the $5,000 she claimed it would take to get her out of the mess. The next day the judge reduced the charge to disturbing the peace and fined Belle five dollars.

But the sympathizing cattleman got something for his money. To show her gratitude Belle threw him a three-day party in her hotel suite. Even after realizing he had been hoodwinked by the Bandit Queen the cattleman seemed well satisfied with his investment.

After the celebration Belle rode out to where the German was trying to rebuild his store, apologized and gave him a thousand dollars, then warned him he'd better turn "Reb."

A few weeks after the trial Belle went to Arkansas to visit her daughter, Pearl. She stayed about two months, doing some deep and serious thinking. She loved and missed her children, but with her reputation they could never live with respect in Dallas. And Dallas was changing: the citizens had voted out her sheriff and other friends in a recent election. Belle's "laws" were replaced with a reformed government.

When Belle started to return to Dallas she told her relatives she was going to close out her affairs and leave Texas for good. True to her word she stuck strictly to business when she returned, selling her livery stable, farm and other holdings, turning all her assets into cash. She kept out of sight, not visiting any of her old hangouts. However, a few days before she planned to leave, the new sheriff arrested her on a warrant for horse stealing.

With her friends out of power Belle knew she was in deep trouble. Eventually with her money she was certain she could stay out of prison, but she would probably be broke. There had to be another way. And she found that way. One of the deputies was fascinated with the Bandit Queen. He spent most of his time hanging around her cell, lusting. Her cell was isolated from the rest of the jail. Belle took full advantage of the man's desires, by inviting him to spend a night with her. During the night she talked him into freeing her and eloping, even though the deputy had a family.

Belle sent the deputy for her rig, packed with all her personal belongings which she had stored at a friend's, who also stabled the strapping team of thoroughbreds she planned to drive to Arkansas.

The big thoroughbreds could fly. Belle and the deputy soon had many miles between them and Dallas. As soon as her disappearance was discovered a big posse was formed and fanned out looking for the Bandit Queen. Two days later the lawmen found the deputy tied to a tree at a crossroads. Pinned to his chest was a note: "You can have him back. Proved unsatisfactory."

The deputy told a story that a gang of outlaws took Belle from the jail at gunpoint and kidnapped him. However, no one put enough faith in the story to file escape charges against Belle.

A few days after her escape from the Dallas jail Belle arrived in Conway, Arkansas. She began making future plans. A good home for her children was top priority.

But before she could give much thought to her plans a friend brought bad news. Cole, Bob and Jim Younger, Frank and Jesse James, Sam Wells, Clell Miller, and Bob Stiles tried to hold up a bank in Northfield, Minnesota. The ill-fated robbery attempt took place September 7, 1876 and turned into a nightmare for the outlaws. At last the gang had met its match. A furious gunfight errupted between the townspeople and outlaws. The bandits didn't get a dime and were shot to pieces. Outlaws Stiles and Miller were killed, all three Youngers wounded, yet, somehow in the hail of bullets the James boys escaped untouched. Two days after the robbery attempt the wounded Youngers were captured.

When Belle heard the news the old flame for Cole Younger rekindled. Maybe she still loved him; she didn't know. It didn't matter, the old ties were still there and he was the father of her beloved daughter. The Youngers needed help. She had money, lots of money and knew her way in courts. Without hesitation, Belle caught the next train to Northfield.

As soon as she arrived in Minnesota, Belle hired the best criminal lawyers available. A long drawn-out court fight followed. After several months of wrangling, the defense lawyers got the Youngers off with life sentences instead of hanging.

Belle returned to Conway, Arkansas, happy she had saved her friends from the gallows, but almost broke. Without funds she had to rewrite her future plans. She had to have money, and quickly. To return to Texas was suicide. Her thoughts turned to the Indian Territory. Her friends the Starrs had money and power. Best of all there was no law. That was it; the Indian Territory was made to order for what she had in mind.

CHAPTER TEN

Piece by piece Belle thought through her future. Most important were her children, their education and an opportunity to grow into respectability. She reflected on her own past. Yes, she had been cheated — the war, the dammed Yankees. Still she wanted revenge, and needed money; she would have both.

With a plan of action well organized, Belle rode to the Starrs' domain in the Indian Territory. The Starrs' kingdom in the great bend on the Canadian was ideal for the operation she had in mind: mastermind, business manager and guardian for outlaws. She knew most of the men who rode the back trails of the Southwest and the Indian Territory. Horse and cattle rustling were the big moneymakers if one knew the markets and the ropes. Belle did. Most rustlers didn't; they sold out quickly and cheaply. This was where she would come in, selling the stolen livestock at fair market prices.

To put her operation in motion was simple. Belle had connections both inside and outside the law. First she surrounded herself with a band of bodyguards and enforcers: Blue Duck, Jim French, Jack Spaniard, and of course the Starrs. All were notorious badmen who would lay down their lives to protect their "Queen." Next she set up a spy sys-

tem throughout the region to report the activities
of the U.S. marshals, the only law in the Indian
Territory. Using her spy experience from the war
years, Belle soon had information on every marshal
riding the territory—their habits, strengths,
weaknesses. The ones who could be bought or
threatened, handled by whiskey, dope, or a lady's
charms were catalogued.

Belle worked hard and thoroughly setting up her
operations. She rode throughout the territory
scouting out hideouts for wanted men and stolen
livestock.

The most famous of these hideouts became
known as "Robber's Cave," located about thirty
miles to the south of her headquarters. This big
sandstone cavern deep in the wild San Bois Mountains was an ideal location. Huge boulders and a
cliff formed a natural corral with only one entrance
which could be closed with a pole gate. There was
plenty of fresh water from a spring-fed creek, and
several valley meadows offered lush grass.

With the groundwork laid, Belle went to work.
The first job she masterminded was probably the
"granddaddy" of all horse rustles. Through her
outlaw network Belle heard that the army post at
Fort Dodge, Kansas had received over 200 horses
and that the horses were not to be branded with the
U.S. Brand for several weeks. The thought of two
hundred unbranded horses excited her. At $30.00
each, that would be a lot of loot. The hideout in the
San Bois Mountains would be ideal to hold the big
herd for market.

To handle the job, the Bandit Queen picked Jim
French, Blue Duck, Jack Spaniard, Andrew White
and Sam Starr. The gang rode to Dodge City. Belle
and Blue Duck checked into a hotel as man and

wife using the name Jackson, posing as wealthy Texas cattle-people.

Dressed as a high-society lady, Belle rented a rig and drove to Fort Dodge. She used the same tactic she had used so many years before, posing as a inquisitive, refined lady. She had no trouble making friends with the officers at the fort. Asking innocent-sounding questions, she soon learned the fort's routine.

Every day for a week she paid the fort a visit and made friends with the young officer in charge of the mounts. The young man, trying to impress the charming visitor, proudly showed her his herd of unbranded horses. While the officer talked Belle studied every detail of the post. The horses were being held in a large corral outside the fort. The herd was guarded by a single sentry, with a change of guard at midnight.

One night she rode out to the post, hid in the brush and studied the guards, discovering the midnight-to-daylight guard didn't walk his post. He just sat down, leaned against the fence and slept, feeling sure no one would disturb the army's horses.

With the job thoroughly scouted Belle chose Saturday night, or early Sunday morning, to relieve the army of its mounts. She knew most of the officers and men from the fort would be in Dodge City whooping it up.

Belle sent all the gang, except Blue Duck, riding out of town with orders to wait about a half mile from the fort, saying she and Blue Duck would be along shortly.

While she was scouting the fort, Blue Duck had been sitting in some friendly poker games at the Dodge House run by a gentleman named Bat

Masterson. Blue Duck lost a large amount of cash. This irritated Belle. She was in town to make money, not lose it.

Changing into her buckskin riding gear Belle strapped on a pair of guns and sent Blue Duck around to the back of the Dodge House with their horses. She climbed the back stairs, going down the hallway to the room where the game was in progress, and knocked. A voice said. "Come on in, the door isn't locked."

She kicked the door open. Money was stacked high on a table surrounded by several players. The gamblers froze as they stared through the clouds of floating cigar smoke at the buckskin-clad woman with a gun in each hand. Belle laughed. "All right, boys, see this pair of forty-fours, that's four-fours. Good hand wins the pot, right?" She waved the guns. "Anyone want to argue?"

None of the men said a word, or moved, they just stared. The piercing black eyes leveled over the guns said she would use them. Holstering one gun, she pulled a pillowcase from the front of her blouse and tossed it on the table. "You with the fancy vest, I believe Mr. Masterson is your name, be a gentleman and cram all the money in that bag. Oh yes, and don't go for that fancy gun in your belt."

Masterson no doubt had heard frontier talk about Belle, the Bandit Queen, and probably recognized her. He knew she had the drop on him. "Hurry it up, sack up the money!" she shouted. Masterson didn't argue. "All right, you gentlemen step back from the table, take off your pants and throw them out the window," her voice commanded.

The men hesitated. "Shuck those britches," Belle snapped. The men looked at Masterson. He was already unbuckling his belt. The others followed his lead, and out the window went their pants. She smiled and backed out the door. "Thank you, gentlemen."

Belle gave Blue Duck a good tongue-lashing as they rode to meet the rest of the gang. Driving off the army's horses was simple. One of the men slipped up behind the guard, hitting him on the head with a gun, then tied him to the fence. By daybreak, Belle, her gang, and the herd of horses were in full flight toward the Indian Territory.

The gang took several days driving the herd to the hideout in the San Bois Mountains. The getaway was clean, there was no pursuit. The army was too embarrassed to report the theft to civilian laws.

After securing the herd in the natural rock corral, Belle left her gang guarding the horses and headed for Fort Smith to find a buyer. She started making the rounds of saloons, livery stables and wagonyards, until she found her man—Huggins, a buyer for an army post in Texas.

Belle introduced herself to Huggins as Ruth Tacker from the New Mexico Territory, and said that she had started across the Indian Territory for Kansas with a herd of good horses, but heard there was a better market in Fort Smith. Huggins was all ears and was anxious to ride with Belle to look at the horses. The two headed for the mountain hideout. Huggins looked the horses over, and after some bargaining he agreed to pay thirty dollars a head for the herd, on delivery to Fort Smith.

The horses were delivered as agreed by Belle and her gang. Belle paid her men their share and sent them back into the Indian Territory. She stayed in Fort Smith, now with some operating money. There were things to be done.

As usual when in the chips Belle bought a new wardrobe. Then she started making the rounds of the saloons, bellying up to the bar and drinking with the boys, and getting acquainted. As she hoped, a buzz started around town. During the socializing she was picking up information and asking questions. Her top priority was learning the names of the best criminal lawyers in town; she was sure she would need them later.

After a week of business and pleasure Belle headed back to the Starrs. As she rode there were many things on her mind. Her operations were getting off to a profitable start. Now to unite herself with her children and provide a home for them. But there was a problem: Blue Duck. He had proved disappointing—a good lover, but with a weakness for gambling. Her men had to be strong and tough, no weaknesses. She smiled. There was the handsome Sam Starr, a bachelor, with guts and brains. Plus his family had power, money and land. Sam was her man.

Belle wasted little time in getting rid of Blue Duck. A whirlwind romance with Sam Starr ended March 10, 1880, with Belle and Sam united in a Cherokee tribal wedding.

Before the wedding a friend of the Starrs tried to talk old Tom Starr, Sam's father, into stopping the wedding. The man told Starr of Belle's past and that she was an evil woman.

However, instead of taking the friend's advice, old Tom threw one of the biggest wedding celebrations ever held in the Cherokee Nation. He was proud of his new daughter-in-law; she was full of "wild medicine" and the devil, which would be an asset to the tough Starr clan.

Belle was happy. Starr was the name she needed.

"Belle Starr! Belle Starr!" She repeated the name over and over. She strutted like a peacock. The name had romance, color and would attract attention. The newly married couple settled in Sam's home, a two-room log cabin. Sam had done an excellent job selecting his homesite. The cabin was on a rise on the south side of Hi-Early Mountain. The cabin overlooked a small wild meadow. Rimmed by a heavy forest beyond the trees, a bigger flower-splashed meadow rolled down a gentle slope to the blue Canadian River. It was just a cabin, quite a step down from Belle's usual luxury, but she loved it. The place was home.

There was only one entrance to Sam's homesite. That was through a brush-and-boulder-lined shallow canyon. To approach the cabin without being detected was almost impossible. Belle delighted in everything about her new home. It was perfect. The protected location couldn't have been planned better. She spent hours gazing out across the scenic wilderness.

Once settled in her new home Belle took charge. She bought curtains, furniture and other decor in Fort Smith. With the cabin furnished, she brought her daughter Pearl from Conway, Arkansas, deciding to bring her son Eddie from Missouri later.

The cabin wasn't a mansion, but it was a home. With her daughter settled in, Belle started enlarging her business operations. She built several additional cabins near by. These were to house her outlaw friends, a real robber's roost.

Belle was proud of the kingdom she was establishing, but her headquarters needed a name to glamorize Belle Starr. After some thinking, she christened her new home in the great bend of the

Canadian, "Younger Bend" after Cole Younger. Sam Starr didn't mind, Cole Younger was his friend.

One of the first visitors to use Belle's Younger Bend facilities was Jesse James. He was using the name Howard and posing as a Baptist preacher. Jesse stayed around several weeks riding the countryside, which was full of U.S. marshals on the prowl.

Life was now once again beautiful for Belle. She had her beloved daughter, a home, and a tough, handsome husband. Every minute possible Belle spent with Pearl. They rode the beautiful primitive wilderness, picking berries, wild fruit, picnicking and visiting neighbors.

They did most of their visiting on the south side of the Canadian River. There was a good reason. The Canadian River was the boundary between the Choctaw and Cherokee Nations. Younger Bend, Belle's headquarters, was on the north side of the river in the Cherokee Nation. A short distance to the west was the Creek Nation.

Belle did thorough research on the population of the region when she settled. She discovered that a much finer class of whites lived south of the Canadian River in the Choctaw Nation. These few whites had a fair education and seemed to have higher morals than the whites on the north side of the river. The Choctaws were much better citizens than the Cherokees and Creeks. Belle only associated with outlaw Creeks and Cherokees. The Choctaws were deep sympathizers with the Southern cause during the Civil War, not split as was the case with the Cherokees and Creeks.

The whites in the Choctaw Nation had several things in common with Belle. Most had fled the

South to escape the Yankee reconstruction oppression, and all wanted a better life for their children—education, respectability, and high morals.

While Belle had a high regard for the whites on the south side of the Canadian she had a very low one for those on the north side. In a letter to a relative in Conway, Arkansas, she gave this evaluation of the whites on the north side: "The women aren't fit for breeding and the men are a bunch of pig-stealing apple-knockers."

Belle and Pearl ranged far and wide in the Choctaw nation. They became friends with some of the most prominent Choctaw families, the Leflores, McCurtains, Walkers and many others. The two spent much time visiting in the nearby communities of Whitefield, Enterprise, Hoyt and Brooken. Belle helped to establish some of the first schools for whites in the region.

The schools were of a subscription type. A traveling teacher would come into the area and offer to organize a school, charging so much per student. The classroom was usually a church or the living room of a home. Most residents of the area were hard up for cash. To get a school started Belle in many cases put up a cash advance guarantee to the teacher, so Pearl could advance her education. In her Younger Bend home Belle stocked a classical library and a piano.

CHAPTER ELEVEN

Belle's power and notoriety spread. She enlarged her operations to include illegal whisky-running and control over prostitution in some of the mining camps in the Choctaw Nation.

While her business ventures were prospering and expanding, Belle's activities were also attracting the attention of none other than Issac C. "Hanging Judge" Parker in Fort Smith.

On Sunday, May 2, 1875, Issac C. Parker stepped off a steamboat at Fort Smith, Arkansas carrying with him a United States appointment to the judgeship over the Western District of Arkansas. At thirty-six, Parker was the youngest Federal judge ever appointed, and assigned the toughest task ever to face a judge. The new judge didn't only have authority over Western Arkansas, but also over 74,000 square miles of Indian country to the west (now the state of Oklahoma). Roaming this vast wilderness where there were no "white man's courts" rode soldiers of fortune, killers, thieves, robbers, whisky peddlers and other flotsam of society. Many were victims of the Civil War forced into a life of crime, others had chosen their own destiny.

Fort Smith was a town of twenty-five hundred people when Parker arrived. He and his family expected much more than they found in the way of comfort, luxury, progress and social life. They soon discovered Fort Smith was the wildest town on the frontier.

Crime and vice ran openly with no regard for the law. The place was the playground for every thug and desperado west of the Mississippi, drawn by the country's largest red-light district and by the numerous gambling halls.

On his arrival Parker encountered another problem. He was a hated damned Yankee, and was given to understand that good and bad citizens alike didn't trust "a Northern carpetbagger."

However, it didn't take Judge Parker long to show he was from a different mold than his predecessors. The new judge set up headquarters in the commissary of the old fort. And eight days after his arrival he opened his first term of court. Eighteen suspects were tried for murder, fifteen found guilty, eight of which the judge sentenced to death by hanging. The executions were to be carried out September 3.

One of the condemned men's sentence was commuted to life imprisonment. Another was shot and killed trying to escape. The remaining six were to keep their date with the noose. The upcoming mass hanging attracted nationwide attention, fanned by the Eastern press. On the morning of the executions a crowd of over 5,000 gathered. Workmen had been working for a week constructing a gallows, a crude but strong wooden structure, a ten-foot-high platform with a 12-by-12 I-beam suspended on sturdy studs above it. In the floor of the gallows were traps twenty inches by four feet, which if sprung at the same time, could plunge 12 men side by side to their deaths.

At 9:30 A.M., the six condemned men, Daniel Evans, William Whittington, James Moore, Smoker Mankiller, Sammuel Fooy and Edmond Campbell were led from their cells and walked to the gallows surrounded by an escourt of guards. The curious crowd pushed and shoved trying to get a better look at the condemned men as they climbed the rough steps of the platform. The felons weren't allowed quick executions. First they were seated on a bench at the back of the platform. Then for the lusting crowd the show started. Hymns were sung and several ministers of different faiths offered prayers.

After the good words each prisoner was asked if he would like to make a last statement. Some gave long heart-rendering speeches; others said little or nothing. It took about two hours to get through the preliminaries, then the six condemned were lined up on the trap doors, black hoods pulled over their heads, and rope nooses tightened around their necks by George Maledon the infamous hangman. At a signal from a deputy marshal Maledon pulled the trigger to the trap doors and the six men plunged simultaneously to their deaths, then swayed, limp heaps of carnage before the eyes of the curious.

Next day headlines across the nation screamed disgust at the disgrace of public mass executions. Judge Parker was called a heartless, sadistic butcher in many of the news stories.

The judge didn't personally attend the executions, but watched from a window in his courtroom.

After the first mass hanging Judge Parker's next order of business was to appoint two hundred deputy U.S. marshals to police the Indian Territory with orders: "Bring them in alive—or dead."

Many of the men appointed marshals carried records worse than the men they were to hunt down. They received their pay on a commission basis, so much per arrest, with an average pay of $300.00 per year, unless they picked up some reward money. The low pay scale left many open to the temptation of bribes and payoffs, Belle Starr's speciality.

Judge Parker's court was unique in the United States in that it actually, in some cases, had more power than the United States Supreme Court. Parker's court possessed the first original and final jurisdiction, final being irrevocable. He could deny new trials and appeals. With this power to back him, Parker handed out his own form of justice. He stood firm in his belief that "The wicked must pay, and he would judge who was wicked."

To support his form of law and order Judge Parker hand-picked his own jurors. A group of "Parker's Pimps" hung around his court and survived on jury-duty fees and other handouts. It was hardly unusual for rigged evidence to be used in the prosecution of a wanted man.

This was the type of law Belle had to deal with when she established her headquarters at Younger Bend.

Belle Starr's name kept cropping up in Judge Parker's court, and he became highly curious and rankled. Although the accounts varied, the Judge gathered Belle was riding high in the saddle in the Indian Territory. She was called the ruling queen of his domain to the west. He judged her a "she-devil" who must be brought to the foot of justice. So the word went out from Judge Parker, "Bring in Belle Starr."

Belle was tipped off that the judge was after her. It was not unexpected, they were natural enemies. She didn't worry, she had built plenty of insulation between herself and her criminal activities. However, the Bandit Queen underestimated the judge.

One July morning 1882, Belle and Sam sat on their horses at the head of the canyon which led to their home. They noticed a horseman riding across the meadow toward them. "Do you recogonize him?" Sam asked.

Shading her eyes from the sun with her hat, Belle squinted hard. "Yes, it's Marshal Captain Marks."

Sam's face hardened. "What the hell do you think he wants?"

"Relax, Sam, he's one of the few marshals that's worth a damn. He isn't a bounty hunter. He is honest and never looks for trouble."

Marks rode nearer. He spotted Sam and Belle, then pulled up his horse. Belle shouted, "Ride on up in the shade, Marks."

The marshal walked his horse up beside Belle and Sam. "Hot as the devil," he said, taking off his hat and fanning his brow.

Belle said, "You are so right, Marshal," then turned to Sam. "Captain Marks, this is my husband, Sam Starr."

After the men exchanged greetings, Belle asked, "What brings you out our way?"

Marks suddenly realized he had ridden into a trap. He was between Sam and Belle. He knew their reputations. His eyes played back and forth between the two, then lingered on Sam's guns. Belle read the marshal's nervousness and prodded, "Something wrong, Marshal?"

Marks knew he could be shot the minute he answered. But he didn't back down. "Belle, I have a warrant for your and Sam's arrest."

Sam's hand inched toward the big forty-five on his hip. Belle's eyes narrowed. "A warrant, what the hell for?"

Marks tensed, his breath short and heavy. He

didn't have a chance if Sam and Belle decided to resist arrest. There was only one chance: he felt Belle respected honest lawmen. Looking her straight in the eye he said, "It's for horse stealing."

Belle snapped. "And whose horses are we supposed to have stolen?"

Marks shifted slightly in his saddle, keeping his eyes on Sam's gun hand. By reputation Sam Starr was the fastest and deadliest gun in the Indian Territory; if anyone was faster it was his wife, Belle. Marks knew he had to be frank and honest, pick the correct words or die. "You are charged with stealing two horses. One from a boy named Crane, the other from a man named Campbell."

The tension broke, and Belle threw back her head and laughed. "Well, I'll be damned! You must be kidding, Marks."

Belle was as relieved as the marshal. Even though her criminal activities were well covered, she thought the arrest warrant might be for some big deal. She laughed again. "Marks, so your great Judge Parker has finally trumped up some charges against us. I heard he was trying."

Sam, who had been silent, cut in. "Hell, at least they could have accused us of stealing some good horses. That old nag of a mare of Campbell's is one-eyed and winded, and that little old pony of Andrew Crane's wouldn't make good crow bait."

"Come on, let's ride up to the house. It will soon be lunchtime, I'll fix something and we can talk this deal over," Belle said.

Marks didn't like the idea, but knew he had no choice. Belle fried some venison and warmed up some beans. After they ate she told her daughter Pearl to go outside. "Marks, I respect you as an honest lawman. But you are the biggest damned fool in the world to ride into a trap like this."

Marks was nervous; maybe he had played his hand too far. And maybe he had underestimated Belle. Had he been led like a sheep to slaughter? He had to talk fast. "You say you didn't steal the horses. In that case why would you want to kill me?"

"You're right, Marks, I have decided we will go peacefully and make a fool out of your great Judge in court." Belle paused and stared hard at the marshal. "Remember, we are going, you aren't taking us. And we will have to go by way of Hoyt so I can leave my daughter with some friends."

Belle packed some things and Sam saddled a pony for Pearl. They rode through the canyon with the marshal in front. As they approached the Canadian River two riders burst from a willow thicket with leveled Winchesters. Marks recognized Jack Spaniard and Blue Duck. "Put your hands up, Marshal," Spaniard snapped.

Marks started to obey, but Belle stopped him. "Lower your guns, boys, everything is all right. We're going on a business trip to Fort Smith with Mr. Marks." She winked at Sam. "You boys ride and tell Daddy Tom to meet us there, we might need him."

Pearl was left with friends. Belle, Sam and Marks continued the seventy-odd-mile trip to Fort Smith. They spent the night in a camp near Keota. The marshal was actually the prisoner.

Next day when the three arrived in Fort Smith about noon, old Tom Starr was waiting, just as Belle had requested. Sam and Belle were arraigned before U.S. Commissioner James Brizzolara and pleaded not guilty. As Belle expected, they were bound over until the next term of court and their bonds set at $2500 each. She had the money, but didn't want to post the bonds lest it would arouse suspicion as to how she acquired so much cash. So Tom Starr posted the bonds.

After their release, Belle retained the two best criminal lawyers in Fort Smith, Cravens and Marcum. She was determined to get the case dismissed during the preliminary hearing, to avoid being heard before Judge Parker.

However, Belle's plans went awry. Commissioner Brizzolara specified in his court order that Belle and Sam were to be brought to trial before none other than Judge Parker.

The day of the trial, February 18, 1883, the courtroom was jammed. The notoriety of Belle Starr, "Queen of the Outlaws," had been spread by sensational news stories throughout the nation. The attorneys Cravens and Marcum moved that the charges be dismissed. They made a strong case that the Federal Government had no jurisdiction, since all involved were Indians, and the case should be tried in the Cherokee courts. Judge Parker overruled the motion. Belle was a white woman regardless of her intermarriage status. With Cherokee law to back them up Belle's lawyers continued to hammer away on the legal issue, but Judge Parker overruled motion after motion.

Newspapers across the country gave the trial front-page coverage with banner headlines screaming "Outlaw Queen before Hanging Judge, for Horse Stealing."

The prosecution presented evidence that Belle and Sam led the two horses in question to John West's place, asked and received permission to leave them overnight, and sometime the next day they returned and took the horses.

The defense endeavored to show that John West, the only eyewitness, was actually the one who stole the horses and that he schemed to save himself from the law. The defense established that Belle and Sam were not in the vicinity on the date of the alleged theft.

During the trial Belle took notes and advised her attorneys. When she was called to the witness stand she kept her composure under a barrage of questions from the prosecution. Over the objections of the defense attorneys Belle was forced to tell much of her past. The prosecutors hammered. She was the ex-wife of Cole Younger and Jim Reed, and an expert with guns and horses.

The prosecution's case was based entirely upon circumstantial evidence and character assassination. The defense was strong, sound and flawless. But Belle lost confidence as the trial progressed. It became apparent that she and Sam were not on trial for horse stealing, but for who they were.

Expecting the worst, Belle sent her daughter Pearl to relatives in Kansas. Her fears were correct: Sam was found guilty on one count of horse stealing and sentenced to one year in federal prison. Belle was found guilty on both charges and sentenced to six months on each count. This meant they would both spend the same amount of time in prison. If they were model prisoners they would receive three months off.

Belle swore until her death she and Sam were framed. To her it was another case of "dammed Yankee" justice. Her lust for revenge boiled as Judge Parker pronounced the sentences. He had won a battle, but not a war. Belle vowed to bring him to his knees, embarrass him, make him squirm, and destroy him.

The trial and prosecution of Sam and Belle Starr set off a string of bitter feuds among the Starrs and the West clan, Belle, and Judge Parker.

On the day they were sentenced, Sam, Belle and twenty other prisoners were loaded onto a train and sent to the Federal House of Corrections at Detroit, Michigan. Again bold headlines screamed, "Belle Starr, Outlaw Queen, Sent to Prison."

Before she was loaded onto the train Belle wrote a letter to her daughter Pearl expressing her deep love and apologizing for the humiliation she was bringing to her children. Also, she tried to explain that the institution wasn't a prison, but a school. And that the year in the school would allow her needed time to do some studying and writing.

Belle and Sam were model prisoners. Belle shunned notoriety and quickly adjusted to prison life. Because of her education she was put to work in the prison office keeping records. To her surprise she discovered the female prison personnel with whom she worked were just one step above illiteracy. Soon she realized some of the officials were resentful and jealous of her superior education.

Fearing that some of the jealous personnel might cause her trouble, Belle asked to be transferred to regular prison routine. The request was granted and Belle Starr, the "Queen of the Outlaws," was assigned to a group learning to weave cane seats for chairs. Soon the nimble fingers, which could do tricks with cards, fire a gun with lightning quickness and play a piano, mastered the art of chair-seat weaving. Belle had only one thing in mind, to serve her time and go back to her home at Younger Bend.

On November 21, 1883, Belle and Sam were released from prison. Belle told many friends that this was the happiest day of her life. The two were given ten dollars, an outfit of cheap prison-made clothes, and placed on a train to Eufaula, Creek Nation, Indian Territory, the nearest rail stop to their home at Younger Bend.

Three days later Belle and Sam arrived in Eufaula. They were greeted by Sam's father Tom and several other members of the clan. Before they had boarded the train in Detroit, Belle had been given permission to send old Tom a telegram asking him to meet the train in Eufaula with suitable clothes, horses and money. Tom brought Belle's favorite outfit, her flashy buckskins. After a joyful greeting, old Tom and the rest of the clan headed back to Younger Bend, leaving Sam and Belle to do a little celebrating. They rented a room in the Forest House and spent the next week on a second honeymoon.

When Sam and Belle arrived at their home in Younger Bend the first thing Belle did was to send for her daughter Pearl. Then she started putting her business operations back into order.

When everything was running smoothly Belle and Pearl started renewing old friendships south of the Canadian River. They were welcomed with open arms. Their neighbors, and the people who knew them best, believed Belle hadn't been guilty of the horse theft for which she was convicted, and that she and Sam had been trapped. Belle was considered a good neighbor and friend who would go out of her way to help people.

Belle also had the reputation of being the best veterinary in the region. Her lifelong love for horses and years of experience raising and training them gave her a deep knowledge of treating their illnesses and injuries. To broaden her knowledge she studied all available material on horse breeding, care and treatment. And she always kept a good stock of veterinary supplies.

When it came to nursing a horse the weather was never too foul, or the night too dark for Belle. A neighbor named Belt, south of the Canadian River at Brooken, bought a high-blood stallion. One cold winter day while running and playing, the fine horse slipped on the frozen ground and broke a leg. Belt was going to shoot the animal, but a neighbor suggested he go across the river and get Belle.

As usual Belle came in a hurry. Several men were gathered when she arrived. With the men's help she moved the stallion to a barn stall. Following Belle's instructions the men fashioned a swing with chains, straps and ropes, and fastening the swing to barn rafters, the horse's forelegs were raised. Then Belle splinted the broken leg with palings from the garden fence. Several weeks later the leg mended and Belt sold the stallion to Belle.

Belle was just as good at nursing humans as she was livestock. As with veterinary supplies, she always kept a cabinet stocked with human medical needs. And she knew more home and Indian cures than anyone in the region.

Dr. Bonds of Canadian twenty miles to the southwest was the only physician in the region. So Belle was called upon frequently to practice her skills in caring for the sick and injured. Due to her many years of riding the outlaw trails her skills at treating the injured were remarkable, said Dr.

Bonds. He said she was more skilled at treating wounds and setting broken bones than many physicians, and that many people owed their lives to the Outlaw Queen.

Dr. Bonds first met Belle when Pearl had pneumonia. Belle rode to Canadian and asked the doctor to ride to Younger Bend and treat her daughter. Bonds only knew of Belle by her reputation and was surprised at her education. After Pearl's recovery the two became very close friends and when in the Younger Bend area, the doctor usually visited Belle. Many times he asked and received her assistance in treating cases.

After Belle and the doctor became friends she and Sam were in Canadian and stopped by Bonds' office to pay him a visit. When they entered they found the doctor being threatened by a drunk who owed a bill. Belle and Sam listened a minute. Then Belle jammed a gun in the drunk's back and made him pay. Then she marched him out into the middle of the street. There Belle and Sam started making music around the drunk's feet with their sixguns with Belle singing, "Hop up, yellow dog, jump a little higher, hop up, yellow dog, your tail is in the fire!"

CHAPTER TWELVE

Even though Belle appeared carefree and happy, she wasn't the same woman who had been sent to prison. The woman who returned was the revenge-crazed teenage girl, the one that rode with Bloody Bill Anderson, the intense hater waiting for a chance to strike. She hid her emotions as she schemed and planned her attack on Judge Parker. He had humiliated her, and he was going to pay as so many other men had done. She planned her attack, as only Belle Starr could, and her full arsenal of weapons would be thrown at the judge: sex, education, political connections, bribes, even the gun if necessary. He was going to squirm and crawl before she was through.

A few months after her release from prison Belle took Pearl to Fort Smith on a shopping trip. They arrived late in the evening, put their horses in a stable, then checked into a hotel. As they started upstairs to their room Belle noticed an Eastern newspaper on a rack. The headline read, "Belle Starr, the Bandit Queen, Back Home At Younger Bend." She bought one of the papers and folded it under her arm so Pearl couldn't see the headline. Late that night after Pearl was asleep Belle read the article. It was mostly fiction telling of her release from prison as a glamourous, ruling queen

riding herd on a court full of Robin Hood outlaws.

The writer never knew it, but his article gave
Belle the course of action for which she was
searching to launch her attack on Judge Parker.
The press was conditioning the country for a real
Outlaw Queen. They wouldn't be disappointed, they
would get one. Yes, her fame and notoriety would
spread from coast to coast, from Canada to Mexico.
Her previous activities would be child's play com-
pared to what she was thinking of. Openly she
would defy the law. And she would not go to jail
again. She would make a goat out of Judge Parker
and expose him to the world for the sadistic devil
she believed him to be.

Belle slept little the rest of the night. Excitement
gripped her as she laid her plans. Next morning
she took Pearl to some friends' home, saying she
had some business to look after and would return
for her daughter in a few days.

With Pearl in good hands Belle went to her
dressmaker. If she was to be a queen, she must
dress like one. Leaving the dressmaker, she visited
a saddle shop and bought a handmade silver-
trimmed sidesaddle. The saddle wasn't quite fancy
enough to suit her taste so she had more trim
added.

A few days later Belle strolled from her hotel,
swung into the silver-mounted saddle strapped on
the back of her big black stallion, Midnight, and
made her queenly debut. Slowly she rode west
along Garrison Avenue, the silver-trimmed saddle
glistening in the sun, complemented by the new
black riding habit which clung to her body, pulled
even tighter by the silver-studded gunbelt around
her waist. Nestled in the holster was the silver-

plated forty-five, a gift from Cole Younger when he was sent to prison. All the finery was capped by a new white Stetson cocked at just the right angle to show the everpresent ostrich plume.

People on the sidewalk stopped and gazed at the striking lady riding along the street. Belle twirled her quirt and smiled. Now and then she would make Midnight rear up and prance about on his hind feet. A crowd followed.

After several blocks Belle stopped in front of a saloon. With queenly grace she dismounted, tied Midnight to a hitching post, and walked through the batwing door. Most of the men in the crowd followed. The women shook their heads and scattered.

Inside Belle paused and let her eyes adjust to the dim lights and smoke, then stepped up to the bar. "Give me a glass of Red Raven. And set 'em up to the house," she shouted, slapping the bar with her quirt.

The customers, the bartender and the ones who had followed her inside blinked. Belle whacked the bar again. "Get with it, my good man! You must have never been asked to serve royalty before."

The wide-eyed bartender looked out at the crowd as if for help. Belle snapped, "Sir, I ordered a drink of Red Raven and drinks for the house."

Still blinking, the bartender turned, selected a bottle from the mirrored back bar, set a polished glass in front of Belle. His nerves were unstrung, and he missed the glass with the first tip of the bottle. "Steady up, man," Belle encouraged.

On the next try the bartender's aim was on the mark. Belle picked up the glass and smiled. "Now to my guests," she motioned at the onlookers with her quirt. "And one for yourself."

The men pushed up to the bar and were served their calls. Several formed a semicircle around their hostess, wondering about her identity. Raising her glass high and smiling, she cried, "Here's to your health, gentlemen. And drink lively, it's on me. Fix 'em up again, bartender."

Belle was doing what she liked best, acting. She bowed, smiled and touched glasses with those nearest her. Then suddenly her face turned hard. The merriment in her eyes was replaced by the devil. It was a face at the back of the crowd. There was no mistaking that pinkish bald head, big eyes and vein-broken face. They belonged to one of the jurors who helped convict her, one of Judge Parker's stooges.

Her eyes drilled the man. His face flushed redder. He knew she recognized him, and began trying to inch toward the door. Belle fought back her anger. The smile returned. There was a better way. "Hey you, agatehead! You're not leaving! Come here, you sweet little bastard!"

The man paused and the crowd turned toward him. Sweat popped out on his forehead. Belle twirled her quirt. "I said come here." Her voice was cold, commanding. The man looked about for help. But the hushed crowd pushed backward, blocking the door. Belle crooked her finger. "Come here, agatehead, like a good little son of a bitch."

Belle continued to twirl the quirt. "Come on, little man." There was no escape. The man staggered forward. Those cold black "she-devil" eyes had him locked. The man's eyes were fixed with fright. He moved closer to the menacing quirt, hypnotized. The crowd hushed. Then suddenly Belle lunged forward, throwing her arms around the frightened man's neck. The man tried to duck away, but the strong slender arms pulled him close and tight.

The man struggled and moaned, "Please. . . ." His feeble voice was smothered by Belle's lips on his. She pressed her mouth hard and caught his under lip between her teeth, bit until blood oozed. Her clipping teeth moved up and nipped blood from each ear. Then the man was shoved backward. "Now you little bastard, go tell your great Judge Parker, that the Queen of the Outlaws expressed her love to you for sending her to prison."

The man took to his heels. Belle turned and scanned the crowd, then threw back her head and laughed. The crowd roared with her. Taking a leather pouch from a pocket in her skirt she shook out some gold coins and pitched them on the bar. "These are for the drinks. And the show was free." She waved her quirt, bowed and strutted through the doors.

Before returning to Younger Bend, Belle made sure most of the population of Fort Smith either heard of or saw the Bandit Queen. She systematically visited cafes, saloons, theaters and even Judge Parker's court. On her visits to the Federal Building she made more than just chance acquaintances with some of the officials. Some of the more important ones were invited to her hotel room. Part of the entertainment included her picking their brains for information about Judge Parker and the activities of his marshals.

With her public relations work done, Belle took Pearl and rode back to Younger Bend, now sure of herself.

CHAPTER THIRTEEN

Soon after her queenly debut in Fort Smith, Belle's public relations work began to bring dividends. One morning a distinguished visitor, Mr. Charles M. Cook of Fort Smith, came calling on her in Younger Bend.

Cook was one of Judge Parker's court officials. Fort Smith was preparing to host a county fair and Mr. Cook was chairman of the entertainment committee. He had dreamed up the idea that if he could persuade Belle to bring some of her friends to the fair and pull off a fake stagecoach robbery the grandstands would be packed. "Belle Starr, Queen of the Outlaws, and Gang Robs Stage." That billing would insure the fair to be a success.

Belle was delighted at the idea. It would give her a chance to act and gain more notoriety. But she played hard-to-get. She would only put on the act under one condition: Judge Parker must be a passenger in the stagecoach. Cook, knowing Belle's hatred for the judge, didn't like the idea. He offered Belle money and other concessions if she would forget about the judge. But she held firm: no Judge Parker, no act.

In desperation Cook agreed to talk to Judge Parker and give Belle an answer in a few days. The judge agreed and the show was on. Cook rode back

139

to Younger Bend and worked out the deal with Belle. The fair was to run for four days, October 14-18. Belle and her gang would stage the robbery all four days, and receive two hundred dollars expense money paid in advance by Cook.

Cook hurried back to Fort Smith, elated. With any kind of publicity the fair wouldn't only be a success, but the biggest attraction ever offered in the region. He went to work with handbills, billboards, and newspaper notices. "BELLE STARR, OUTLAW QUEEN TO LEAD OUTLAWS AND INDIANS IN REAL-LIFE STAGE COACH HOLDUP." The ads went on to read, "See Belle Starr, former wife of notorious outlaws Cole Younger and Jim Reed."

Many newspapers picked up on the notices and ran the story as front-page news. The night before the fair was to open, Belle, Sam and their gang of outlaws and Indians rode into town. They put up their horses, then began making the rounds. Belle was in all her glory leading the gang from saloon to saloon. She was a real queen, and acting the part. Before they started the tour, Belle laid down the law to her gang: they must conduct themselves as gentlemen."

Crowds followed Belle and the gang from one saloon to another, and business boomed.

The next day the grandstands were jammed with an overflowing crowd all waiting to have a look at the glamorous Outlaw Queen and her band of outlaws. Just as advertised, at 2:00 P.M., the stage pulled on to the half-mile tract in front of the grandstand. Belle followed on Midnight. After a loud colorful introduction by Cook the crowd responded with a wild ovation as Belle waved, and pranced Midnight about on his hind legs.

Next Belle's gang rode on to the track behind

their queen. The stage driver cracked the whip. The horses sprang forward. Belle and her gang dashed in hot pursuit yelling and shooting. Most of the gang were standing high in their stirrups firing rifles over their horses' heads. No one, including the driver of the coach, was sure the gang was firing blanks. As the wild bunch bore down on the coach the driver lost his cool. He jumped from the flying coach, leaving the frightened, racing horse driverless.

When the driver bailed out Belle held back her gang, not letting them overtake the runaway coach, but the shooting and yelling continued. The runaway turned into a wild stampede, the coach swaying and rocking behind the frightened horses. On the turn going into the back stretch of the track the coach skidded broadside and almost overturned, spilling the passengers from their seats. The passengers including Judge Parker panicked, causing the coach to rock and weave even more.

The crowd was on its feet shouting and screaming their approval. Belle wasn't about to disappoint her fans. As the runaway coach skidded through the last curve into the home stretch in front of the stands, Belle waved her gang forward. The outlaws dashed up alongside the coach, knocking out windows and blazing away. Now, many in the stands decided Belle and her gang weren't acting, but were playing for real. Women screamed, some fainted, others made a run for the exits, thinking they were witnessing a real massacre.

When it appeared Judge Parker and the other passengers inside the coach were doomed, Belle and Sam closed in on the runaway horses and grabbed the lead horses' bridles, pulling them to a halt. The gang moved in and pulled the frightened passengers from the coach. Belle dismounted with guns drawn and ordered the passengers to empty their pockets on the ground. She holstered one gun, then picked up the wallets, watches and other valuables and dumped them into her saddlebags. With the job complete, Belle jumped on Midnight, bowed to the crowd and dashed from the fairgrounds followed by her gang shooting and yelling.

Belle was riding high in the saddle as she headed back to Younger Bend. Part of her mission had been accomplished—Judge Parker was embarrassed. Relishing her sweet revenge she turned all her attention to expanding her business operation. Life was beautiful, she was in the limelight and established as the Queen of the Outlaws.

Feeling secure, Belle made a trip to Missouri and brought her young son Eddie Reed to Younger Bend. At last she had provided her children a home and had the money to give them all the advantages. Both her children were enrolled in a subscription school at Whitefield.

Not only did Belle enroll Eddie and Pearl in school, she also hired a private music teacher. Belle worked hard at trying to be a good mother, but she had too much time on her hands. She grew restless; even masterminding her outside-the-law activities didn't fill her craving for excitement. Her activities were profitable, but too tame.

One day a small-fry outlaw, Tooker Davis from Texas, visited Belle at Younger Bend. Davis was running from a bounty hunter, was broke and needed some money and a fresh horse. Belle, always in sympathy with a man on the run, helped him. In return for the favor he told her where there was a large roll of money just waiting to be picked. Captain Sam Brown, Euchee Chief and Treasurer of the Creek Nation ran a store in Lenard, a small settlement about fifty miles northwest of Younger Bend. The Chief kept the Creeks Treasury in a safe at the store. Davis planned to rob the Chief, but the bounty hunter was breathing down his neck.

Belle spent a week checking out Davis' story. Finding it true, she gave a thorough scouting to surrounding terrain and back trails for a safe and fast getaway.

On a cold frosty November morning in 1884, two strangers rode up to Brown's Store. One was white, the other Indian. They tied their horses to the hitching rail and sauntered inside.

Captain Brown was talking to a customer named Childers when the two entered. There was a brief friendly greeting and conversation between the men. Then the strangers pulled their guns and demanded the money. Childers tried to argue and was knocked out by one of the men with the butt of a gun. Brown, after being threatened, opened the safe. The bandits stuffed the money in a canvas bag, tied up Brown, then rode off. It was a big haul of $6,000.

Soon after the bandits left, Childers regained consciousness and untied Brown. Brown rode hard and fast and soon had a large Creek posse hot on the trail of the robbers, but lost their trail in the hills a few miles southeast of Checotah.

Belle underestimated Brown. He wasn't as dumb and spineless as she had guessed. Instead of making big noise and then quitting, the Chief sent a telegram to the Federal authorities in Fort Smith requesting help. Judge Parker assigned several deputy marshals to the case. After much investigation, and from the description of the bandits by Brown and Childers, warrants were issued for Sam

Starr and Felix Griffin, charging them with robbery.

Led by Captain Marks, a small army of marshals descended on Younger Bend. Captain Brown and his posse of Creeks insisted on riding along. They were up in arms over losing their treasury and had an intense hatred for the Cherokee Starrs.

Marks was against the Creeks riding with him. He was afraid Brown and his posse might touch off a violent fight with the Starr clan. Marks knew his only chance of arresting Sam without a fight was to talk with Belle, and the presence of the Creeks wouldn't help.

Marks tried to reason with Brown, but the Chief and the other Creeks were determined. They felt highly insulted at Marks' suggestions and wouldn't listen. Marks decided to change his plans and wait a few days and see if the Creeks would disperse and go home. But the Creeks were worked up to a fighting pitch. They made it plain that they were tired of Marks' stalling, and if the marshals didn't go in after the Starrs, then they were going by themselves.

The marshal was in a quandry. There was nothing to do but go ahead and ride into Younger Bend. He couldn't let the Creeks go by themselves. He was sure they would touch off a battle, perhaps a tribal war.

So against his better judgment Marks, his marshals, and the Creeks rode toward the entrance to the canyon which led to Belle and Sam's home. The marshal was sure his every move was being watched over rifle sights. Near the mouth of the canyon, Marks stopped and held a conference. Again he pleaded with the Creeks to wait and let him ride in alone. Again Chief Brown wouldn't agree, repeating the threat that he and his posse would go with or without the marshals.

Desperately, Marks worked out an agreement with the Creeks. He would take Brown and four other Creeks, the rest of the posse and his marshals would wait. The marshal was doubtful the plan would work. But he couldn't make the Creeks understand that once they rode inside the narrow canyon, they were sitting ducks. The Creeks didn't know the Starrs as the marshal did.

Followed by the Creeks, Marks rode into the canyon. The marshal cursed under his breath. Chief Brown was too stubborn for his own good. The lawmen rode only a short distance when Belle appeared, stepping from behind a big boulder, with a rifle leveled. "Hold it, Marks! Where in the hell do you think you and that bunch of blanket-ass Creeks think you are going?"

Marks stuck up his hands, palms outward. "Belle, I need to talk to you."

Belle inched closer. "What the hell about? Come on, spill it. Spill it."

"It's bad, Belle. I have a warrant for Sam and one for Felix Griffin."

"What the hell for?"

"Robbing the Creek Treasury at Lenard."

Belle looked past Marks at Chief Brown. "Well, well, so the poor dumb-ass Creeks lost their scully. And they think Sam took it." She laughed. "Wrong, marshal, Sam is in Webber Falls and has been there for a week, and can prove it."

Chief Brown shouted. "She lie! She lie! Sam Starr robbed us."

"Oh hell," Marks said under his breath. "The fat's in the fire now." Just as the marshal suspected, several rifle barrels appeared suddenly from behind boulders and trees. The Winchester barrels were all the marshal could see, but he knew men were behind them. The click of cocking hammers told him that.

Marks watched Belle's eyes narrow to slits. Her voice was like ice. "One more word out of you, blanket-ass, and your hide won't hold water."

At last the truth of the situation got across to Chief Brown. His eyes moved about the ring of gun barrels which were fencing him in, then back to Belle. Belle paid him no more attention, turning to Marshal Marks. "Marshal, Sam isn't here. Like I said, he's in Webbers Falls. I haven't see Felix Griffin in several days."

Belle paused and moved closer to Marks. "Now marshal, if you don't want to take my word and want to ride up to my house and look around, you're welcome."

Marks thought a moment. Belle might be telling the truth and she might not be. That wasn't the question. She was trying to set up a trap. Not for him, but for the Creeks. If she could get him away from the scene the Creeks were going to be gunned down on the spot. That was her game. He was sure.

"No thanks, Belle, I'll take your word."

The marshal turned and motioned at the Creeks. "Let's go, men."

Chief Brown and the Creeks turned their horses and followed. They didn't argue this time.

Belle shouted after the men. "Hurry back, Marks, when you are by yourself and have more time." Marks turned and waved.

When the lawmen were out of sight Sam stepped from behind a big boulder and laughed. "That marshal has his hands full with those Creeks."

Belle replied, "Yes, but I'm afraid we have our

hands full with that marshal. I don't think he was fooled, Sam. I think you better go on the scout until things cool off."

With Sam on the scout Belle settled down to spend more time with her children, and keeping up with the social life south of the Canadian River.

It was fall, a romantic time in the isolated rural area. There were many square dances and play parties. Belle loved the parties and dances.

The party games were nothing more than square dances, with one exception. The difference was music and a caller. In party games the couples went through the routine swinging and dancing to the rhythm of their own singing. And like square dancing calls, the party games had names—Chase the Buffalo, Old Dan Tucker, Roll That Ball My Darling Girl, and many others.

Many people frowned on square dances, wouldn't allow one in their home, nor attend one, because of religious beliefs. But play parties were accepted.

Belle was always at the top of the list of those invited to dances and parties. She was also a good hand at "getting up a party." This took a lot of work and organizing. The custom was to do some family a favor: cutting wood, harvesting crops, or some other type of chore. As a reward for the favor the family would then entertain the community with a dance or party.

There was another reason Belle was usually invited to most social affairs south of the Canadian River. Many families were afraid to hold social gatherings for fear the toughs from the north side of the river would show up and cause trouble. However, if Belle was one of the guests, the ruffians either didn't come or behaved themselves if they did. They learned from experience, some the hard way, that Belle wouldn't stand for their rowdyism. She was a good peacemaker, even though her methods were a little rough.

One night in fall of 1884, Belle arranged a dance at the Ed Bryant family's home in Brooken. It was a cold night. Those who were not dancing stood in a semicircle around the fireplace.

Near midnight two uninvited guests from Brairtown rode up. One was Jack Bane, a self-styled tough and notorious troublemaker. Bane was drunk and just as soon as he entered the house he walked over the the fire and started shoving people to one side. "Let the mean old bear into the fire," he snorted.

Belle was dancing. She stopped, walked to the fireplace and carefully selected a stick of wood from the roaring fire. It was a long slender stick, ablaze on one end. Then she took deliberate aim and whacked Bane across the top of the head. "Now turn the old bear out," she laughed.

Bane fell to his haunches. His partner took a step toward Belle with his fist cocked. She punched him in the gut with the fiery end of the stick. "The next poke is going up your rear, if you don't take that bastard and get the hell out of here!" she shouted.

Bane staggered to his feet, blood running from beneath his smashed hat, and followed by his friend, wobbled out the door. Belle followed, prodding the two along with her fiery wand. The two lost no time in mounting their horses and racing into the night.

CHAPTER FOURTEEN

Near Christmas in 1884, someone introduced John Middleton to Belle. Middleton, 25, was a hard-core outlaw. A dangerous killer type, with the Texas lawmen hot on his trail, the young outlaw needed a place to hide and had ridden into Younger Bend.

As always, before she became closely associated with an individual, Belle probed into his past. She checked Middleton out through her network.

In her investigation Belle learned some interesting facts about the young outlaw. He was a close relative of her dead husband Jim Reed. He was a braggart, continually boasting of his bloody escapades while riding with Billy the Kid in New Mexico, and his adventures while riding with the Charley Bowdre gang.

Belle checked out his claims and found most of them to be more or less true. John Middleton was quick on the trigger and a heartless killer. Belle sat down and had a long talk with the young outlaw.

Middleton claimed that the year before he had tried to quit the outlaw trail and settle down. He moved in with his mother and brothers near Paris, Arkansas. He bought a farm and started a crop, but a few weeks later was arrested on an old Texas warrant and locked up in the Scott County, Arkansas, jail. He set fire to the jail and escaped.

A few days after his escape Middleton said he was captured and charged with arson, but escaped again, then recaptured and escaped the third time. After the last escape he killed Tim Thomas, the only witness to the arson.

After the escape and murder Middleton drifted back to Texas. He bragged that a few months later in November, 1884, he shot and killed a Texas Sheriff, J.H. Block, in a gunfight. That was when he headed for Younger Bend with the lawmen on his trail.

Belle listened to the young outlaw's story with interest, skepticism and suspicion. There were several things which didn't quite add up. His claim that he had ridden a short time with the Youngers, she didn't believe. She was certain she would have heard him mentioned. There was no doubt, Middleton was a wanted man, but she was suspicious. He was up to something other than hiding from the law.

Middleton was tough, a killer, but also treacherous unless Belle missed her guess. She didn't trust him. Yet, she decided to allow him to stay around. He wasn't too smart and could be used. She had something in mind that Middleton would be perfect for.

Robbing Indian treasuries was a very profitable, exciting business, Belle decided. She had inside information that the Seminole payroll would arrive by train in Eufaula shortly after the first of the year, 1885. It would be loaded onto a stagecoach headed west for Sasakwa, where the money would be turned over to the chief for distribution.

Belle scouted out the route and layout, planning

to relieve the Seminoles of their money. It would be an easy job. On the day the money arrived in Sasakwa, Belle, Sam, John Middleton and Grant Cook were waiting.

The stage was protected by a large armed guard of Seminoles. While the Seminoles milled around watching the strongbox unloaded, Belle and her gang sat on their horses off to one side, unnoticed.

The strongbox was carried and set on a platform in front of a store. The crowd followed. Suddenly Belle spurred her horse into the Seminoles and plucked a baby from its mother's arms, whirled and dashed away. Thinking it was a kidnaping the Indian guards and most of the other men gave chase. Belle let the big thoroughbred she was riding have his head, easily outdistancing the Seminoles' ponies.

About a mile from town Belle pulled up the big horse and let the posse overtake her. She bowed and smiled at the stern-faced men with drawn guns, then handed the baby to one of the Indians and explained the whole affair was just a joke. The relieved Seminoles just stood, nodded and returned Belle's wave as she rode off.

Several miles away Belle met her gang, who had lifted the strongbox while the Indians were chasing her. The frustrated Seminoles formed a posse, but failed to pick up the trail of the bandits. There was much talk about the robbery, but no warrants were ever issued.

Sam Starr and Grant Cook hit the owlhoot trails again after the robbery. Middleton was bolder, he hung around Younger Bend. Talk spread that with Sam in hiding, the young outlaw and Belle were having an affair.

In the meantime John Middleton moved his

mother and three brothers, Ike, Bill, and Jim, from Arkansas to a farm at nearby Briartown. Belle made friends with the family and was a frequent visitor in their home, always asking questions about John. By adding up the bits of information she gathered from John Middleton's unsuspecting family, Belle decided the young outlaw was out to get her, to avenge Jim Reed's death. He was either going to kill her, or entrap her for the law on a promise of immunity. Belle went to one of her trusted lieutenants, this time Jack Spaniard.

Spaniard followed Middleton's every move, day and night. After several days Spaniard reported to Belle that Middleton was meeting with a Texas Ranger. That was all she needed to know.

That night Belle rode to Sam's hiding place and some plans were made.

Belle pretended to fall head over heels in love with John Middleton, telling him she was tired of Sam, a dumb-ass Indian. Middleton was her kind of man, smart, tough and handsome. In a few days the young outlaw was strutting like a peacock.

Middleton never suspected and was more than ready when Belle suggested that they elope. He got a big laugh out of Belle's scheme to get rid of Sam. Sam was a fool like Belle said. In fact, such a big fool, he was going to help them elope. Middleton was beside himself.

Belle convinced Middleton that she had made Sam believe that she was taking the children on a vacation to Arkansas, and Middleton had agreed to ride along as a guard. Sam would accompany them to Whitefield, then turn back.

The elopement date was set for May 5, 1885. Middleton should have become suspicious. The day before Belle told him he would have to furnish his own horse, that it might look suspicious to Sam if he rode one of hers. Instead of buying a good horse as Belle suggested, Middleton stole one that night. It was a real nag, an old one-eyed work mare which belonged to a farmer, A. G. McCarthy.

Stealing the mare from McCarthy almost stopped the elopement. McCarthy was a friend of Belle's. She started to jump Middleton, but fought back her temper. A fight would wreck her plans.

Next morning the small caravan pulled out of Younger Bend. Belle and her children were in a wagon, Middleton rode in front with Sam following. At Whitefield Belle kissed Sam goodbye and said she would see him soon. Middleton laughed.

The first night on the trail Belle, her children and Middleton camped near Keota. The next morning the party split. Belle directed Middleton to take a back trail which circled to the southeast around Sugar Loaf Mountain, explaining the law might be trailing them.

Two days later a cowboy named Tally found a saddlemare tangled in some brush in the Poteau riverbottoms near the Arkansas state line. The cowboy worked the mare loose and led her to nearby Pocola. No one knew the mare branded with an A on the hip. This caused several men including Tally to wonder about the owner of the mare.

A search party was formed and the next day the body of a man was found near where the mare had been tangled in the brush. Half the face of the badly decomposed body was torn away, apparently by a shotgun blast. There were two guns strapped about the waist and some personal items found in the dead man's pockets. Tally took the guns and personal items to Fort Smith and turned them over to the federal authorities. After a close examination of the articles and from the description of the corpse, it was decided the dead man was John Middleton.

At the same time Tally was in Fort Smith, McCarthy rode in to report the theft of his mare, and said he suspected John Middleton of stealing the mare. He knew the outlaw by sight and said he could identify the body if it was Middleton. Several marshals went with Tally and McCarthy to Pocola.

In the meantime the citizens of Pocola, not knowing what else to do with the badly decomposed body, buried it.

The next day Texas Rangers, Captain Gunn, John Millsap and John Duncan stopped Belle and her children near Russelville, Arkansas. The Rangers seemed surprized that Middleton wasn't traveling with Belle. Their actions confirmed Belle's suspicions about John Middleton. After questioning Belle briefly the lawmen left. Returning to Fort Smith the rangers learned that Middleton's body had been found.

The Texas lawmen then rode to Pocola. Riding with them was Captain John West, a Cherokee tribal lawman, and a cousin of Sam Starr. Taken to the grave by local authorities, the rangers opened the grave and John West positively identified the body.

The Texas Rangers then rode to Russelville and located Belle. When they told her of Middleton's death she called them liars. The lawmen then showed her the outlaw's guns. After inspecting the guns Belle agreed to ride back to Pocola with the rangers.

The body was once more exhumed. Belle said there was no doubt the dead man was John Middleton. She bought a casket and had the grave marked.

A week later Belle and her children returned to Younger Bend, where her loving Sam was waiting. Whether Belle's suspicions about Middleton were correct didn't matter, he was out of her life forever.

The Texas Rangers and other lawmen said openly that Belle had led Middleton into an ambush.

CHAPTER FIFTEEN

Belle didn't spend all her.time fighting Judge Parker and harboring outlaws. Among other things she was a maker of fine wines. Her reputation for making good vintage from the many varieties of wild fruits, berries and grapes which grew in Younger Bend was well known.

Belle once told an eastern news reporter, "Contrary to wild tales, which I myself am responsible for, I drink very little. Sure, I put on a show for the boys in saloons. But the bartenders are paid well to mix my favorite drink, water colored with tea." Most of Belle's close friends confirmed she drank little alcohol.

To make her wine, Belle used an old German recipe. It was given to her father by a German emigrant who worked for him in Missouri. She usually kept a good supply of aged wine on hand, just for very close friends.

One cold frosty January morning someone told Belle her old friend Joe Blake was ailing with a cold. She thought a lot of the old man whom she called "Grandpa Joe." Taking a bottle of her best wine she decided to ride to the old man's home near Brairtown and check on him.

When she arrived at her old friend's place, no one was home. Worried, Belle rode into Brairtown and checked at a store. The store owner told her Blake was much better and had gone to spend the day with a relative.

Belle rode back to Blake's home and left the bottle of wine on his front porch with a note, then headed for home. When she was about a hundred yards away from Blake's house, she glanced back over her shoulder and saw a man crouched over, slipping through a cornfield.

Pulling up her horse Belle watched the man. He was headed toward Blake's house. She reined her horse out of sight behind some cedar brush, then dismounted. The man stopped at the edge of the field and looked around. Belle recognized him as one of the Hayes brothers. The brothers were a pair of illiterate hillbillies from Arkansas. They lived by themselves on a small rented farm and were notorious petty thieves.

Belle watched Hayes slip toward the house. No doubt he had seen her leave the bottle of wine and was going to steal it. Ground-anchoring her horse, she slipped back through the brush toward the house, until she was about twenty-five yards away, watching Hayes. He would creep forward about ten feet, then pause and look around. He would make "a damned poor Indian," Belle laughed to herself. The last few feet the thief sprinted, scooped up the bottle and fled to a gully behind the barn.

Belle was sure Hayes would hide in the gully and gulp down every drop of the wine so he wouldn't have to divide his loot with his brother. They were both gluttons. And Belle also knew that the wine carried a heavy alcoholic content and that by drinking it fast, the man would be thoroughly drunk by the time he reached home. She went back to her horse, mounted up and rode around the countryside for awhile, then headed toward the brothers' home.

The sight that greeted Belle at the Hayes home was even a better show than she had expected. The wine thief was leaning against the side of the house gagging and puking. Between heaves he beat the wall, yelling and cursing his brother. The brother was circling, shouting, "You're crazy! You're gone crazy!"

There was no yard fence, and Belle rode up to a few feet of the brothers. She watched a few minutes, then shouted, "What in the hell is going on?"

The sober one whirled, his eyes wide with fright. "Archie, he done gone caught something awful, Miss Starr. Help me with him. He's gonna die for sure."

Belle swung from her horse and walked closer to the drunk. She studied him a moment, then turned to the other brother. "Ed, I'm afraid, in fact I'm sure, Archie is going mad. Been bit by a mad dog, I guess."

Ed turned white and started wringing his hands. "Oh, my God, no, what can we do?"

Belle turned to her horse and pulled her Winchester from the saddle boot. "Not but one thing you can do for a mad dog."

Ed fell to his knees. "No, no, please Miss Starr, don't shoot Archie. He's all I've got. Maw and Paw are dead, jest me and Archie. Ain't there something you can do? I've heard you are good at doctoring folks."

Pretending to be in deep thought, Belle lowered the gun. "I know an old remedy that might work.

Saw it cure hydrophobia on a bull yearling once. Since Archie is all you have, I guess it would be worth trying."

Ed cut in. "Archie ain't got that high stuff, too, has he, Miss Starr? You said he was going mad."

"Same thing, Ed."

Archie interrupted the conversation with a fit of gagging and heaving. He fell to the ground, rolling and flailing. "Please, Miss Starr, please, do something quick, Archie is going," Ed pleaded.

Belle was now fighting to keep a straight face. "Guess we better, before we have to shoot him. But we must act fast. Because just as soon as the fits leave him he will head across the country biting everything he meets, people, cattle, horses, dogs, cats, even hogs." She paused. "Now, Ed, you're going to have to help me treat him."

"Don't worry, Miss Starr, I'll do anything to save Archie."

Belle put the rifle back in the saddle boot. "First, we have to make sure he doesn't have any food or water for three days. The only way I know to do that is lock him in your corn crib. That might cure him." She took Ed by the shoulders, looking him straight in the eyes. "Ed, now, are you sure you will do exactly as I say?"

"Promise, Miss Starr, promise on a Bible."

"All right, Ed." She mounted her horse and started shaking out her lasso. "I'll rope and hogtie him. I can't take a chance on him getting away, or biting us." Archie was up holding his stomach and reeling about, and Belle pitched her quirt to Ed. "Now wade in on his back with that. I can't make a good sure catch unless he's on the run."

Ed caught the whip and looked at Archie, then back at Belle.

"Dammit, Ed, fly in on him, if you want to save him. Otherwise I'll just shoot him and get it over with. That would probably be best anyway."

"No, no, Miss Starr, you promised."

"Yes, and you promised to help. Now make up your mind. Either start laying it on him, or I'll shoot."

Ed circled the hurting Archie. "Hurry up!" Belle shouted.

The frightened Ed swung the whip. It lashed and bit hard into the heaving Archie's bowed back. The sting of the quirt cut through Archie's miseries enough to jump him into a run. Belle yelled, "Stay after him, Ed. Lay it to him, he 's not running fast enough yet."

Ed was warming to the task and was giving Archie a good beating. They circled the house and as they turned a corner with Belle in hot pursuit on her horse she threw a loop. As the rope settled around Archie's shoulders Belle's trained horse stopped and jerked the rope tight. Archie flew in the air, landing hard on his back. Belle jumped from her saddle with a pigging string in her mouth. Running down the rope rodeo style she threw a quick whooie on Archie, then threw up both hands. "Pretty damned fast time, Ed."

Belle called her horse forward to loosen the rope, pulled it from the hogtied man and fastened in back on her saddle. "Now, Ed, catch Archie by the feet and drag him to the corncrib."

The crib was a small, ten-by-ten foot, dovetailed log structure, with a clapboard roof, plank floor, and a heavy wooden door secured by a piece of chain and padlock. Belle helped Ed toss the hogtied Archie inside amidst some scattered corn and shucks. Then she jerked loose the pigging tie, slammed the door and snapped the padlock. "Now give me the keys, Ed."

"They're in the house, Miss Starr."

"Hurry up, go get them."

Ed dashed into the house and returned with the two keys tied on a string. "Is this all the keys?" Belle asked.

"Yes, ma'am."

"I'll be back in three days. And, dammit, don't you poke any food or water through the crack. Because if Archie bites you, then I'll have to shoot you both, understand?"

"Yes, ma'am."

Just as promised, three days later Belle rode back to the Hayes brothers' place. Ed ran to meet her, shouting. "My God, Miss Starr I'm glad to see you! I sure think Archie is cured."

"Why, Ed?"

"For two days he has been begging and praying for water. Said he's on fire."

"Slipped him any?"

"Oh no, done jest like you said."

"Let's go see if he's cured," Belle said, swinging from her horse.

As they neared the barn Archie started yelling. His voice was hoarse and dry. "Sound like he's cured, Miss Starr?"

"I don't know, sounds pretty bad."

"He sounded better last night. I couldn't sleep for his taking on."

Belle stopped in front of the crib door. "Ed, he might make it, if you can keep him away from water the rest of the day. Think you can?"

"Yes, ma'am, I'll do anything to help poor Archie."

"All right, it's up to you," Belle said, fishing the keys from her pocket.

"My God let me out, I'm dying," Archie shouted.

Belle snapped open the padlock and jerked the door open. Archie bolted through the door and headed straight for the Canadian River, about two hundred yards' distance. Belle shouted, "My God, Ed, head him off. If he gets to the river he's a goner."

Ed dashed in hot pursuit. Belle jumped on her horse and joined the chase, yelling and shooting in the air. For a short distance Ed seemed to gain on Archie. But Archie glanced over his shoulder and ran harder. He wasn't about to be caught. Belle held back her horse just enough to stay a few yards behind Ed. "Get him, Ed, get him! Don't let him get to that river!"

Ed tried, but wasn't fast enough. Archie didn't break stride as he dived off the high riverbank into the icy water. "Jump in and get him quick, Ed," Belle shouted.

Ed hit the cold water a few feet behind Archie. Archie came up and started swimming for the opposite bank with Ed in pursuit. Belle threw back her head and laughed, then whirled her horse and headed for home.

CHAPTER SIXTEEN

1885 saw the Queen of the Outlaws reach the peak of her power. In her years at Younger Bend, Belle had established a large empire of hundreds of acres of land. Grazing the land were large herds of cattle and horses wearing the Belle Starr brand. Her many illegal ventures were prospering as well—selling stolen livestock, running whisky, and managing brothels. With her inside connections she was keeping herself and her confederates out of Judge Parker's court. The queen was riding high in the saddle.

Early in 1886 Belle got the opportunity to challenge Judge Parker's power. Blue Duck, her former lover and good friend, was going on trial before Judge Parker, charged with murdering a farmer.

The trial ended January 30, the verdict exactly as Belle expected. Blue Duck was found guilty and sentenced to hang. In pronouncing sentence, Judge Parker went into a long discourse on "the evil which must pay." Belle was sitting in the courtroom. Judge Parker wasn't sentencing Blue Duck, but her. She decided to show the judge who had the power. Blue Duck would not hang. He was framed, innocent of at least this murder, Belle knew.

For three years Belle had been laying the foundation for just such a power confrontation. She was ready. The Hanging Judge was going to eat crow.

She would attack the judge from a source he would least suspect and from one he would be powerless against.

Two years before, during Grover Cleveland's successful campaign for President, Belle had been contacted by an Eastern politician, James Hartman. Hartman explained Cleveland had a good chance of winning, but needed funds, big money, to fight the rich Republican bloc. It took little coaxing to get Belle interested, since she hated all Republicans. During the discussion Hartman promised Belle White House favors if she ever needed them. Now she was going to find out if the promises would be kept.

Belle had gone about her job as fund raiser with all her crafty ability, using all her tools—blackmail, bullying, and female charm. She visited several wealthy people in Arkansas, Texas and the Indian Territory. Large amounts of money poured into Cleveland's campaign coffers. There have been estimates that Belle Starr may have raised a quarter of a million dollars for Cleveland.

The President was the only one with power to override Judge Parker's decisions. Blue Duck would not hang; Cleveland owed her a favor. She would go to Washington to visit the President of the United States.

Early next morning Belle was in Eufaula dressed

as a young man. She was disguised to prevent Judge Parker from learning her plans. Before boarding a train for the East she sent a telegram to her friend Hartman in Kansas City asking him to meet her train.

Belle spent two days in Kansas City. True to his word Hartman, by wire, arranged for her to visit with Cleveland. Before boarding a train for Washington she bought a wardrobe of the latest fashions.

The visit with the President was a success, Cleveland agreed to review Blue Duck's case.

Belle returned to Younger Bend in high spirits. She was confident Blue Duck's sentence would be commuted to a life sentence. Then she would laugh in Judge Parker's face.

She won. Two weeks before Blue Duck's date with Judge Parker's gallows, the judge received a written order from President Cleveland commuting Blue Duck's sentence to life imprisonment. Later he was pardoned. The Hanging Judge was furious. Belle strutted around Fort Smith letting the world know the Bandit Queen had given the judge a lesson.

However, Belle had little time to relish her victory over Judge Parker. Sam had quit the owlhoot trails and had returned home. The U.S. marshals had lost interest in catching him, but not the Cherokee Police. Cherokee Sheriff Vann was determined to arrest Sam and Felix Griffin for robbing the Creek's Treasury.

One March morning in 1886, Sam was riding along the south end of Hi-Early Mountain, looking for stray cattle, when he saw Vann and a posse riding toward him. They had him cut off from home, so he so all he could do was make a run for it. He was certain his thoroughbred could out-distance the posse's horses. Whirling the big horse around he headed up the north side of the mountain. Then he saw more riders in the brush on the crest. They had him surrounded. There was only one way out of the trap. He had to get across the Canadian River to the south side and safety.

Sam headed straight for the river, the posse in hot pursuit, sure their prey was cornered. A thirty-foot-high bluff formed the north bank of the Canadian; that would stop his escape.

For protection, just in case the posse started firing, Sam swung to the side of his racing horse, one hand gripping the saddle horn, the other holding a six-shooter. Now and then he snapped off a shot across his horse's neck at the pursuing lawmen.

Hearing the shots, Belle mounted a horse and raced to the scene. Seeing the posse closing in on Sam she pulled her Winchester ready to launch a counterattack. Then she realized Sam's intentions. He could do it on Wildwind. She had raised and trained the big horse. She pulled her mount and watched.

The posse didn't return the fire and slowed their horses. They were sure Sam was fenced in, his escape route closed. He would have a choice, either to surrender, or try to shoot it out and be killed.

Then in disbelief, the posse watched Sam straighten in the saddle and stick his spurs to his horse. The big horse responded by increasing his stride. Racing toward the high bluff, Sam hooked his spurs under his horse's belly and leaned forward and low in the saddle. The posse pulled to a stop. Then without breaking stride the lanky thoroughbred soared into space. For a few seconds horse and rider silhouetted against the sun, then splashed into the blue water. Both submerged, then surfaced and swam for the opposite bank.

The horse and rider scrambled up the low sandy south-side bank. Sam turned and waved and disappeared into the dense brush. The bluff from which Sam jumped his horse now forms the north anchor of the Lake Eufaula Dam.

Belle doubled with laughter at the helpless, shocked posse who shook their heads in disbelief. Raising her Winchester she fired a couple of shots. The posse whirled, Belle thumbed her nose, then stuck the spurs to her horse.

Felix Griffin, the other suspect in the Creek robbery, wasn't as slippery as Sam. He was a tough customer, fast with a gun, whose speciality was highjacking whisky runners that didn't pay Belle for protection.

Belle was standing on her front porch one afternoon when another of her men, Jack Spaniard, rode in. "Who's after you, Jack?" she asked.

"A marshal just captured Felix Griffin at Brairtown."

Belle arched her eyebrows. "Know the marshal?"

"Bill Irwin."

"The double-crossing bastard," Belle snapped. "Took my money, now he's let Judge Parker push him into a double cross. Never should have trusted Irwin, the weak skunk."

"What are we going to do about Felix?" Spaniard asked.

Belle's eyes narrowed to slits. "We can't let Irwin get to Fort Smith with Felix. It's up to you, Jack."

Marshal Irwin didn't ride to Fort Smith that night with Griffin. Probably fearing trouble and an ambush he made camp near Whitefield. Early next morning the marshal started out with his prisoner. The two took the old Whisky Trail with Griffin handcuffed to Irwin's saddle.

Near Newman, Marshal Irwin and his prisoner met Dump Shorpshire. The marshal asked Shorpshire if he had seen any strange riders in the area.

Shorpshire replied he hadn't seen any strangers, but had met Jack Spaniard and Frank Palmer on the trail. This confirmed Irwin's suspicions. He was certain Spaniard and Palmer were setting up an ambush. So instead of continuing east on the Whisky Trail, he veered to the north toward Tamaha. The land, mostly a flat prairie, would make it easy for the marshal to spot riders for miles.

However, someone either tipped off Spaniard and Palmer, or they figured out Irwin's change of plans. The next day the marshal's body was found in the dense brush on the bank of Little San Bois Creek, near Tamaha. He had been shot through the head with a rifle. Again, Felix Griffin was free.

On April 12, 1889, Jack Spaniard was tried and convicted in Judge Parker's court for the murder of U.S. Marshal Bill Irwin. Spaniard was hanged for the crime August 30, 1889.

CHAPTER SEVENTEEN

Early one May morning one of Belle's lookouts knocked on her door. "What's up?" she asked.

"There's a marshal at the head of the canyon, says his name is Hughes. He wants to talk with you."

Hughes was another of the marshals Belle held in high regard, all business and honest. She thought a moment. "Tyner Hughes—all right, let him ride in."

Belle waited on the front porch. In a few minutes Hughes rode up. "Had breakfast, Marshal?"

"No, I slept in a cold camp last night, Belle."

"Well tie up your horse and come in. I've got some ham, eggs and coffee."

Belle drank coffee while the marshal ate. Neither spoke. When the marshal was finished Belle asked, "Hughes, why am I honored with your call?"

Hughes wiped his mouth with a red bandanna, then took a sip of coffee while putting his answer together. "I have two warrants for you."

Belle smiled. "I've been expecting to hear from my dear, devoted friend Judge Parker. What crimes am I supposed to have committed this time?"

Hughes dug the warrants from his inside coat pocket. Belle's relaxed mood had the marshal worried. He was expecting a tirade and here she was

171

smiling. He unfolded the warrants. "You are charged with stealing a mare from A.G. McCarthy on one charge and helping hold up N.H. Farrell in his home at Choctaw station, the night of February 27."

Hughes got another surprise. Belle threw her head back and roared with laughter. "Well, old Parker is sure scraping the bottom of the barrel this time."

She laughed again. "Funny thing. I was just thinking yesterday that I needed to go to Fort Smith. While I change clothes would you go to the barn and saddle that big bay gelding for me? It will be a privilege to have you as an escort."

The strange couple rode out of Younger Bend. The marshal knew what had happened to Marshal Bill Irwin a few weeks before. Instead of taking the shorter Whisky Trail to Fort Smith he took the back trail along the north bank of the Canadian River to its junction with the Arkansas River. Hughes didn't ride beside Belle. He rode the lead for a while, then dropped back to the rear. At times he circled off the trail left or right.

Everything was going too smoothly. Hughes became more suspicious. He was sure they were being watched and followed. He watched Belle. She seemed happy, bright, and smiling. It just didn't make sense.

As the couple neared the confluence of the Canadian and Arkansas rivers the trail narrowed as it passed through some dense cottonwood trees. It resembled a leafy dark tunnel and forced the riders to ride single file, the marshal behind Belle. Hughes strained his senses. The place was an ideal ambush spot. Belle noticed the marshal's tenseness. "Relax, Marshal. You're safe with me. Nothing to worry a—." Her voice was drowned by the crack of a rifle. A bullet splintered the lawman's saddle horn.

Belle sprang from her saddle and in the same motion whacked the marshal's horse across the face with her quirt. The horse reared and spun, throwing Hughes, as another shot rang out. Belle jerked her six-shooter and dropped to one knee. "Hold it. Whoever you are, you better get the hell out of here, or I'll kill you."

There was a brief silence, then the hoofbeats of a running horse. Marshal Hughes got to his feet. "Belle, you saved my life. Believe me, I'm grateful. Do you know who it was?"

"Hughes, you probably won't believe this, but it was none of my boys. It was probably some young buck trying to build a reputation."

Hughes and Belle caught the marshal's horse. After they were on the trail again Hughes said, "Thanks again, but it doesn't alter anything. I have got to take you to Fort Smith."

"I didn't save your life for favors, Hughes. There are plenty of your kind around that I wouldn't have done the favor for."

Hughes thought of Irwin. Was Belle trying to tell him something? After some thought he decided not to press the issue.

When they arrived in Fort Smith, with Hughes' permission Belle sent a runner for her attorney, William H. Cravens. Cravens met her at the Federal Court, where she was arraigned, pleaded not guilty, and was released.

After the arraignment and posting bail Belle checked into a hotel. She was going to be in town for a while. She was determined to bring Judge Parker to his knees. The charges were so false and trumped-up she was positive that even Parker's court wouldn't convict her. This time she was going to make him the laughingstock of town. It was going to be her show.

To set up her show Belle sent telegrams to the Eastern press. The press reacted beautifully, by condemning Judge Parker and his court. "Tyranny," headlines screamed. "Is there anyplace on earth, even half-civilized, that gives one¹ man the power to charge and try people on personal whims without hope of appeal?"

Belle had another stroke of luck. By chance she ran into Arkansas Senator James K. Jones, a political friend. Jones had been called home from Washington on some important personal business. After a meeting with Belle in her hotel suite the Senator went back to Washington and launched a campaign denouncing Parker and his court.

Taking the Senate floor he spoke for an hour, calling Judge Parker's court "a shame and disgrace to American civilization."

Belle was in a happy mood when she left Fort Smith and rode back to Younger Bend, holding all aces in her battle with Judge Parker. But in a few days after her return home Belle's happiness faded. There was a new problem, from a new source, one which she never expected and a problem with which she didn't know how to deal: her daughter Pearl.

Belle thought she was a good mother to her children. She dreamed and envisioned great futures for them. Uppermost in her mind was to give her children respectability. She ruled son Eddie with an iron hand, but she handled Pearl like a china doll.

By 1886, Pearl was a mature woman of eighteen.

However, her daughter was still a little girl to Belle. Through schooling and Belle's training Pearl developed a charming personality and refined social graces, which set her apart from other young women in the rough country. She attracted attention wherever she went.

Belle loved to show off her daughter. She took her to Fort Smith regularly, dressed in expensive finery, to parade her about town. The pair were frequent visitors to the best theaters and eating places.

But while Belle was teaching her daughter culture and social graces Pearl was learning other things from her mother. When Belle wasn't looking Pearl was using her womanly charms to tease men.

Belle was too busy with her business and other activities to notice Pearl's attention-getting flirtations. Taking advantage of her mother's long stays away from home Pearl started an affair with a young cowboy, Bob Crocker.

Crocker was honest, but shiftless, moving from one ranch to another. All he owned were some flashy clothes, a good horse and saddle. Pearl fell in love with the happy-go-lucky cowboy who came calling when Belle was absent. The courtship went on unnoticed for several months. Then one day the young cowboy rode into Younger Bend and boldly asked Belle for Pearl's hand in marriage.

At first Belle was stunned, then quickly regained her composure and said she had to think the matter over a few days.

Belle's thoughts wandered back to her own starry-eyed youth and her love for the worthless Cole Younger. No, she would never let her daughter suffer the same fate. Pearl must marry a gentleman with social status and wealth.

There were several ways she could stop the wedding and break up the love affair. There was the easy sure way, to have one of her gunslingers take care of the young cowboy forever. That would be simple. Gunfights were many and commonplace the Indian Territory. The winners of the duels were never prosecuted, claiming self-defense. But Belle decided against taking that route. She didn't want to hurt Pearl and she liked the carefree cowboy.

After several days of wrestling with the problem Belle devised what she thought was a surefire plan which would work and not hurt anyone. Using the pretense that Pearl needed to think over her marriage proposal, Belle took her daughter for a visit with relatives at Conway, Arkansas.

Leaving Pearl in Arkansas, Belle returned to Younger Bend, and after a week or two she told Crocker that Pearl had decided against the marriage, and was going to stay in Conway. Taking Belle at her word, the broken-hearted cowboy rode out of the country.

Several weeks later Belle went to Arkansas and brought Pearl home, telling her that Crocker had left for parts unknown. Pearl accepted her mother's story and seemed to forget the affair. Belle relaxed and went about her usual lifestyle.

Soon after the broken love affair a new marshal rode into Belle's place. The Bandit Queen sized up the lawman. He was young, from up north, a real Yankee Doodle Dandy tenderfoot.

Envisioning an entertaining evening at the tenderfoot's expense, Belle invited the young marshal to stay for dinner. Belle acted the part of a gracious hostess and with Pearl's help prepared a fine meal. While cooking the meal Belle served the lawman some of her best wine.

The wine had a heavy alcoholic content, and the hostess continued to fill the marshal's glass. After several glasses the lawman became heady and brazen. He bragged about his prowess as a lady-killer, seeking to impress Pearl. Pearl did nothing to discourage the young man. Now and then she smiled when her mother wasn't looking.

The evening wore on, with more and more wine being served to the marshal. He became louder and bolder. Belle was enjoying the spectacle. The marshal grew wilder with his bragging and his desire for Pearl became uncontrollable. He pulled a large roll of money from his pocket and offered Belle $100.00 if she would allow him to sleep with Pearl.

Belle coiled, her hand darting under her skirt to a derringer, eyes blazing. Then she paused, smiled, looked at Pearl and winked. Turning back to the marshal she said, "Sounds like big easy money, Marshal. It's a deal, if Pearl is willing." She looked at Pearl. "How about it, baby?"

Pearl wasn't for sure what was going on, but trusting her mother, she nodded "yes."

"All right, fork over the money. You pay in advance," Belle snapped.

The marshal counted out a hundred in gold pieces. Belle took the money and turned to a dresser. She deposited the gold in one of the dresser drawers. Then she whipped a mean, short-barreled forty-four from the same drawer and whirled. "Now you Yankee bastard, you can sleep with my daughter, but understand, sleep is all you are going to do. You so much as touch her and I'll splatter your damned low-life brains."

The marshal fought for sobriety. The black eyes leveled over the gun had lost their mirth. Now they were deadly. Belle looked at Pearl. "Go ahead, honey, and get in your bed. This son of a bitch has paid to sleep with you and a deal is a deal."

Then Belle turned her attention back to the frightened marshal, prodding him in the stomach with the forty-four. "Get off those boots and strip to your underwear."

The marshal started to argue, thought better and obeyed. Belle motioned with the gun. "Now lay down on the far side of the bed, Yankee. And you better stay there."

After the two were bedded down, Belle seated herself in a chair at the foot of the bed with the gun on her lap. The marshall didn't sleep a wink. He lay straight and rigid, afraid he might touch Pearl. The odd game lasted until sunup. Then Belle stood and stretched. "All right, Yankee, now you can go back and tell Judge Parker that you not only met Belle starr, but you also slept with her daughter, Pearl."

The summer of 1886 saw Belle's problems multiplying. Things were getting more difficult for Sam. A small army of Cherokee lawmen were making an all-out effort to bring in Belle's slippery husband. But with Belle's and the Starr clan's help Sam was always a jump ahead.

The search for Sam Starr was the biggest in a long history of manhunts in the Indian Territory. Finally several U.S. marshals joined the Cherokee lawmen in trying to capture Sam. There were too many on his trail. He was captured one September evening, in 1886.

A big posse, led by Cherokee sheriff R. P. Vann, deputy Frank West and a Federal marshal named Robinson, spotted Sam riding through a cornfield.

Vann shouted for Sam to halt. Instead he stuck the spurs to his horse. The posse fired a volley. One bullet grazed Sam's head, knocking him unconscious. Another shot killed his horse.

Sam was disarmed and tied, and taken to a nearby house. The lawmen held a conference. They decided to keep Sam at the house until morning. Vann would ride for reinforcements, leaving West, Robinson and the others to guard the prisoner. They knew Belle and the rest of the Starrs would make an attempt to free Sam just as soon as they learned of his capture.

The lawmen were correct. Soon after Sam's capture someone carried the news to Belle. The Outlaw Queen spring into action. A tigress fighting for her mate, she saddled Midnight, armed herself to the teeth, then dashed into the night, alerting the Starrs and her other henchmen.

In a few hours Belle assembled a small army of fierce fighters. Led by Belle the band rode through the darkness and surrounded the house where Sam was being held. When her gunmen were positioned Belle shouted, "Frank West, do you hear me. Either release Sam, or get blown away. I have fifty guns on you." Her demand was backed by several blood-curdling Cherokee yells.

Even though he was a deadly enemy of the Starrs, Frank West was also a relative of the clan. He knew them well. They were fierce fighters who would back down from nothing to save one of their own. But most of all he feared Belle. She not only had guts, but brains as well. West also figured the Outlaw Queen was flanked by her loyal henchmen Jack Spaniard and Jim French. His posse wouldn't have a chance in a shootout with the murderous gunmen. West knew his only chance would be to try and stall until Vann returned with reinforcements. "Belle!" West shouted. "Meet me in front of the house and let's talk."

Belle's voice cut the air like a sword. "The only talking I'm going to do is with my Winchester. West, you have three minutes to turn Sam loose, or you better start praying to save your cowardly soul."

The lawmen held another brief conference. They were trapped. There was no other choice. Sam was released. Belle and her band let out wild yells of victory and fired several shots in the air before they rode off.

Vann took the rescue of Sam Starr as a direct insult to the Cherokee Tribe. He swore vengeance and began organizing an army of lawmen and volunteers to invade Younger Bend and smoke out Sam Starr.

Belle and the rest of the Starr clan were eager to meet the challenge. The fight was more than a personal battle. It was a long, smoldering intertribal feud, deeply rooted in Civil War loyalties. The Starrs had fought with the South, Vann and several of the Cherokee were on the Union side.

The Starr's call to arms brought relatives and allies flocking in from all over the Indian Territory. Fortifications were dug around Sam and Belle's home and at the mouth of the canyon. Younger Bend took on the appearance of a frontier military outpost. To supply firepower some of the Starr gang stole a small cannon, powder and balls from a military train sitting on a siding in Eufaula.

Belle was in all her glory. She took full command, dashing about shouting orders. She had the same old thrill of an upcoming battle. Her mind raced

back to the memory of a wild-eyed young girl
leading Bloody Bill Anderson into battle. Deploy-
ing the guerrilla tactics she had learned so many
years before, she sent out spies to keep her abreast
of every move of the lawmen.

The lawmen were headquartered at nearby
Porum. After a week of preparation Belle's spies
reported Vann and his Cherokee lawmen were
making ready to strike in a day or two. She was
ready. Her plans were carefully mapped. She would
let the invaders enter the canyon, and cut them to
pieces with cannon and rifle fire.

The night before the expected attack Belle did
some thinking. There wasn't any doubt that her
plan of defense would wipe out the invaders. However, she asked herself if it would it end there. Perhaps, like Bloody Bill and Quantrill, she would win
this battle but lose the war. The United States
troops would be called in, and that would end it all.
It would mean the end of her domain, and the
breakup of her dreams, with total surrender.

It was a tough decision. Belle knew she must face
facts. Sam would be eventually killed or captured.
Capture by the Cherokee lawmen meant certain
death. If he surrendered to the U.S. marshals there
was a chance. Weighing all the facts Belle sent a
messenger to Tyner Hughes. He owed her a favor.
She had saved his life. The messenger brought back
word that the marshal agreed to meet Belle on the
south side of the Canadian River and talk.

At high noon next day Sam and Belle were
waiting at the designated location. After a long
conference Sam surrendered to Marshal Hughes.
Accompanied by Belle, the marshal and Sam rode to
Fort Smith. Sam was arraigned on the robbery
charge, bond was posted, and he and Belle spent a

week vacationing in Fort Smith.

Sam's surrender caused a small rift among some of the Starrs, as they had wanted the shootout with the Cherokee lawmen, and felt cheated.

After his release on bail Sam stayed close to Younger Bend. He looked after the ranch and Belle took care of her business operations, and spent much more time with her children.

Things seemed to be straightening out for Belle, even though Sam was facing trial. Then a few days before Christmas she and Sam received an invitation to the biggest social event in the area, Lucy Surrat's Christmas Eve dance at Whitefield.

Belle and Sam took Eddie and Pearl with them, all dressed in their best. Instead of following their usual custom of riding horseback, the Starr family loaded into a spring wagon.

The crowd gathered early for the dance. It was a cold night and a big log fire was built in front of the Surrat home since there was not room for all the guests in the house. The men stood around the fire with the women and children inside.

The musicians were A.B. Cole, a fiddler from Brairtown accompanied on the guitar by Edmond Knowles, a young Choctaw. Occasionaly Belle would relieve the guitarist; now and then she would play the harmonica and give the fiddler a rest.

The men joked and nipped bottles that passed around the fire, and took turns at going inside and dancing. Everyone was in a happy mood. Sam seemed to be enjoying himself. He had brought along a box of cigars, passing them around and wishing everyone a merry Christmas. He was squatting near the fire, lighting a cigar, when Frank West walked up on the other side of the fire carrying a Winchester. West looked the crowd over, and not seeing Sam he asked, "Is Sam Starr here?"

Sam stood and backed away from the fire a few steps. "You looking for me, Frank?"

West didn't answer. Sam said "Frank, you never quit trying." He paused. "You want me real bad, don't you?"

West still made no reply. Sam's voice was calm. "You shot my horse from under me in that cornfield. I surrendered and am under bond. You know that, but still you show up with a Winchester. Frank, this isn't the place and time."

West still didn't answer. Sam said. "All righ , Frank, if it has to be, let's walk out in the road away from these people and settle this thing once and for all."

The two were no more than ten feet apart, just the fire between them. Suddenly West swung his Winchester upward to a level. Sam's hand was lightning as he whipped a six-shooter from his belt. Two shots sounded as one. West dropped in his tracks, Sam's bullet tearing through his throat.

Sam dropped his gun and staggered backward, grasped his chest, clutched a tree, then slumped to the ground.

Belle, hearing the shooting, dashed outside, a gun in her hand. She ran to Sam and knelt. Seeing he was dead she turned and walked over to West who was thrashing about in his death struggles, the blood gushing from his throat. She bent and took a closer look at the wounded Cherokee lawman. She kicked him and swore. "Go ahead and kick yourself to death, you cowardly bastard."

The bullet had gone through West's throat and struck a Choctaw youth named Dan Folsom. The bullet hit Folsom in one cheek, passed through his mouth, and out through the other cheek. Belle caught the boy, who was jumping around holding his mouth. She cleaned his wound with her silk neckerchief soaked with whisky, then ripped a strip from her petticoat and bound up the wound.

Folsom recovered but carried the dimple-like wounds the rest of his life. Later he became sheriff of Haskell County, Oklahoma.

After treating Folsom's wounds, Belle and some men laid Sam's body out in the back of the spring wagon. Then she went back into the house and danced the rest of the night, saying, "This is how Sam would want it."

CHAPTER EIGHTEEN

To everyone's surprise, a few weeks after Sam's death Belle again became a bride. The new husband was Jim July, a twenty-four-year-old fullblood Creek, fifteen years younger than his new bride. The vows were said in Texanna, January 1887.

Belle's new husband was educated, handsome and fast with a gun. These were the qualities the Outlaw Queen most desired in her men. There was a strange quirk to the marriage, other than the age differential. Instead of the bride taking the name of the bridegroom, Jim July became Jim Starr.

While Belle was gaining a new husband she was also gaining some new problems with her children. Pearl was now twenty and Eddie sixteen. Both resented their new stepfather. They had loved Sam Starr. He had been a true friend and the only father they had ever known.

Belle tried to talk and reason with her children, but with little success. Pearl and Eddie stayed away from home as much as possible.

Belle worried about her children. She could see them pulling away, and fretted and fussed about them. Then the big blow came. Pearl had a friend, Mabel Harrison. The girls were nearly the same age and spent much time together. One day the young ladies drove a buggy to Whitefield, telling

Belle they were going after some supplies. This was just a pretense, not the real reason. They wanted to talk to an old friend, Jim Kraft. Kraft was an elderly store owner, very close to Belle and her children.

Late that afternoon Pearl and Mabel returned, followed by Kraft on his horse. Belle was curious about the old man seeing the girls home, but didn't ask. Kraft was invited to have cake and coffee. After some trivial conversation Kraft looked at the girls. "Pearl, would you and Mabel mind going into the other room? I have something personal to talk over with Belle."

By plan the young ladies excused themselves and went to the bedroom. Kraft leaned forward in his chair and lowered his voice. "Belle, I don't know how to tell you this."

Belle eyes hardened. "What is it? What's wrong? Go ahead. You know I won't hold it against you."

Kraft shifted in the chair, trying to find the right words and nerve. But before he could speak Belle made a guess. "Pearl in love again?"

The old man frowned. "No, Belle, nothing that simple." He paused, his gaze dropping to the floor, then in a half-whisper he said "Belle, Pearl is pregnant."

Belle just sat several seconds and stared at Kraft, her stunned thoughts working to grasp the statement. Her baby pregnant? No, it couldn't be. "Mr. Kraft, did I hear correctly, Pearl pregnant?"

The sweat was pouring from Kraft's forehead. He managed a feeble "yes."

Belle shook her head, still not wanting to believe the old man. Then reality caught her. Her baby pregnant! The old hatred boiled. A man, a damned man disgracing her daughter. Whoever he was, the son of a bitch would pay, yes, pay with his life. Then she jumped up and shouted. "Kraft, who is the bastard?" Her voice crackled.

"Belle, I don't know. Pearl didn't tell me."

The old man knew he was face-to-face with a devil ready to release a fury on anything or anyone. "Tell me, old man, tell me! Don't you cover for the son of a bitch."

"Belle, I swear I don't know. Pearl wouldn't tell me, but listen—"

He didn't get to finish. Belle whirled and grabbed the ever-ready quirt from a peg on the wall. He read her intent. "No, no, my God, no. Belle, please!" the old man shouted.

But Belle shoved the old man to one side and dashed into the bedroom, waving the whip above her head. "Pearl, who is the son of a bitch? Tell me! Tell me!"

Pearl cowed back from her enraged mother. Never had she been physically threatened by her mother before. Belle advanced on her frightened daughter. Then suddenly Pearl stopped. The daughter of Belle Starr and Cole Younger, a mixture of those bloodlines, would just back off so far. So sudden was Pearl's stand that Belle was surprised. The two women's eyes locked. Then Pearl leaped at her mother, grabbing the quirt from her grip, and in the same motion swung the heavy end at Belle's head.

Belle ducked the blow. Then, there it was in her hand—that deadly black derringer. Kraft rushed into the room and jumped between the two women. He knew he was facing death, but his voice was calm. "Belle, I won't move. You will have to kill me if you kill your daughter. Listen to me. If you pull that trigger you will hate yourself the rest of your life."

Belle glared at the old man. Then her eyes misted. "Maybe I already hate myself." She lowered the gun. "Pearl, pack your clothes and get out of here. I never want to see you again."

Belle went into another room and returned with a big roll of bills. Tossing the money on the bed she said, "That will keep you off the streets, now get out."

Pearl saddled Blue Bonnet—a fine-blooded mare, a birthday present from Sam Starr—and rode to Fort Smith. There she went to see a friend of Belle's, a middle-aged widower. A whirlwind romance followed. In a week the couple were married.

At best the marriage was a peculiar affair. No one, least of all the prominent bridegroom's family understood his marrying the pregnant daughter of the notorious Outlaw Queen, who was a third of his age.

The marriage was short-lived. Apparently the groom had some plans which he didn't announce before the wedding. No sooner had the vows been read than the new husband demanded that Pearl have an abortion. She flatly refused. Then he suggested Pearl put the baby up for adoption as soon as it was born. Again Pearl refused.

That did it. Pearl left her new husband and went to the Reeds in Missouri. She always thought of her brother Eddie's grandparents as her own relatives. Soon after settling in Missouri Pearl was notified by her husband that he was seeking a divorce and offered her a considerable amount of money if she wouldn't contest the action.

Pearl accepted the divorce offer, and then she

and Grandma Reed traveled to Siloan Springs, Arkansas. Soon after arriving, Pearl went under a doctor's care. On April 2, 1887 she gave birth to a girl which she named Flossie.

As long as she lived Pearl never revealed the father of the child. Rumors floated around that the father was Bob Crocker, Pearl's first lover. He had married and was living in nearby Porum when Pearl became pregnant.

The father of Pearl's child must have been the best-kept secret in the old Indian Territory. Belle searched and used all her many resources trying to scout out the man. She even offered a $500.00 reward for the man's identity. The reward caused several lawmen and bounty hunters to join the hunt, but the culprit was never found. There was one sure bet. The man responsible didn't go around bragging about his conquest.

CHAPTER NINETEEN

A few weeks after Pearl's departure, Belle seemed to have put her daughter out of her mind. Putting her new husband in charge of the ranching operations at Younger Bend, Belle started expanding her business ventures.

Much of her time she spent in Fort Smith. More and more she was making Judge Parker feel her political influence. Many of his previously unchallenged death sentences were now being commuted to life imprisonment by the President.

One hot summer afternoon she was returning by buggy from Fort Smith to Younger Bend by the way of the Whisky Trail when, about halfway between Keota and Stigler, several shots rang out uptrail. Pulling the rig off the road into some dense brush, she stopped and listened. The shooting continued along with some loud yells and shouts. Taking her Winchester, she slipped through the brush to see what the fracas was all about. Getting closer, she could hear some coarse laughter mixed in with the shots and shouts.

Belle moved closer and parted the bushes. What she saw brought a smile. In a wide sandy spot on the trail two men on horses were shooting six-shooters around the feet of a skinny, gangly young man, dressed in overalls and barefoot. The youth was kicking high and handsome as the bullets

191

dusted the hot sand around his feet. It was a real "hoo-raw."

Belle recognized the tormentors. One was a cheap tough from Sand Town, called Slim, the other a petty thief from Tamaha, nicknamed Muley. She watched until the toughs emptied their guns and began reloading, then with Winchester leveled she stepped out of the brush. "Boys, it looks like you're having a really good time."

The toughs whirled, recognized Belle, then laughed. "Well, howdy, Belle, we're shore having us a time. Never seen a tenderfoot jump like this bird," Slim said and pulled a bottle, took a slug, passed it to Muley and laughed. "Think when we empty that bottle we'll see if we can shoot it off the dude's head. So stick around and watch the show."

Belle moved a step closer. "You can bet I'm going to stick around. I wouldn't miss it for the world. Where did you jump this turkey anyhow?"

Muley roared. "Found him hotfooting it along here. Says his name's Harman and he's from Arkansas. Soon as we shoot the bottle off his head, I think I'll make him climb a tree backward. Want to watch him?"

"No, I'd rather see a little swimming in the hot sand."

Both the toughs laughed. "Hadn't thought of that one. Shore glad you come along, Belle. Bet the hillbilly don't know you're Belle Starr, either."

Belle glared at the toughs. "I'll be he doesn't, either. And I'll bet you something else. He doesn't know really how mean I can get, and he doesn't know how ornery I am when I want to have a little fun."

The toughs roared together. "Go ahead, show us something, Belle."

"Oh, I'm going to," she cut in, then motioned with the barrel of her Winchester at the toughs. "Move over there in the shade, Arky." The frightened young man's knees wobbled as he obeyed.

For a moment Belle stood smiling at the wide-eyed youth. Then she cocked her gun and pointed it at Slim. "Now you wanted me to show that kid just how damned mean I am. Well, that is just what I'm going to do."

Slim looked at Belle, then at his buddy Muley. "Both of you buzzards crawl down off those horses," Belle snapped.

"What . . . what you mean, Belle?" Slim mumbled.

"Just what I said. Now get off those horses." She emphasized her command by firing a shot into the air.

"But, Belle we're friends," Slim pleaded.

"Hell, you two cheap bastards are no friends of mine. I said get off those horses."

The toughs looked at each other. Belle fired another shot. That was enough. The two jumped from their horses. "All right, both of you buzzards shuck your clothes."

"What?" the toughs gasped.

"Get out of those clothes, or do you want me to show Arky just how damned mean I am."

Slowly the toughs stripped to their underwear. "Peel off those drawers. I mean, get bare-assed." This time she fired a shot at their feet. The two jumped from their underwear. "Fine, fine, you two are ready for a swim. Now get down on your bellies in that sand."

The toughs hesitated. Belle waved the rifle. "Come on! Come on! Hit it, just like you love it."

Sweat was pouring from the toughs. "Now you don't really mean it, do you, Belle?" Slim pleaded.

She punched him in the gut with the gun barrel. "Hit it. Arky's waiting to see the show." Another jab sent Slim floundering into the hot sand bed. Belle turned on Muley. He didn't need encouragement, he dived after Slim.

Belle moved the rifle to one hand and jerked her six-shooter. A couple of shots in the sand sent the two toughs thrashing about, the blistering sand clinging to their sweaty bodies. "That's the spirit, boys," she yelled and sent another shot near their rears. "Now roll on your backs. Let's have a few back strokes." The tortured men, with arms and legs flailing, turned on their backs. After several minutes and more shots to keep the swimmers lively, Belle shouted, "All right, get out you've had a nice swim."

The relieved toughs staggered from the burning pit, brushing at their bodies and keeping an eye on Belle. "Now you two gentlemen get dressed; get on your horses and ride the hell out of here."

The two just jumped into their trousers, grabbed the rest of their clothes, then dug the spurs to their horses. Belle fired another shot over the fleeing men. "San Bois Creek is two miles up the trail. Take a good swim."

After the toughs were out of sight Belle turned to the frightened young man. "Kid, what's your name? Where you from? And where you going?"

"Silas Harman, from Arkansas, Franklin County, and I'm going to Brooken to see some friends."

Belle smiled. "That is a hell of a long walk. Come on, I'll haul you to Whitefield."

This was Silas Harman's own account of his adventure meeting the Outlaw Queen.

CHAPTER TWENTY

The new year of 1888 brought Belle more personal problems. Daughter Pearl had hurt her, now it was son Eddie's turn.

Eddie, now seventeen, was a strapping, handsome youth, with his father's build and his mother's jet-black eyes and hair. Belle was proud of her son, and as with Pearl she had great hopes and plans for Eddie. She wanted to send him to an Eastern school to study law, but Eddie rebelled—he had other ideas. Belle tried to reason, but their talks usually ended in fights, with her thrashing Eddie with the ever-ready quirt.

With all her intelligence and education Belle never seemed to realize the type of environment she exposed her children to, that they were born into an outlaw society, lived with and were around lawless people all their lives. And somehow she believed that she was keeping her own lawless activities hidden from her children.

Eddie had grown to admire the badmen who hung around Younger Bend. To him the dashing "knights" of the back trails, living by their wits and guns, were idols. He hung around and studied his heroes when his mother wasn't looking. The outlaws were more than willing to teach Belle Starr's son their craft.

Being an eager student, and having astute teachers, Eddie soon became extra-fast and accurate with a gun, and an expert rider with a head full of outlaw survival tactics.

Belle tried to keep Eddie away from bad company, but there was too much around and she was gone too often. Eddie was also hurt deeply by his sister's misfortune and her leaving home. He admired his sister, but felt she had disgraced him.

Before she was forced to leave home, Pearl had great influence over Eddie and her guidance kept him out of trouble. Without his sister's advice, and with Belle gone most of the time, Eddie went wild. He soon began to back his quick temper with fists, knives and guns, earning him a tough reputation. The son of Belle Starr, his father the outlaw Jim Reed, Eddie felt compelled to live up to "his blood." Unlike his sister Pearl, Eddie Reed never used the name Starr, proud of his true name: Reed.

Soon Eddie was becoming involved in one scrape after another, with his mother coming to his rescue. Then he became involved in a whisky-running operation with an older man, Jim Holt. The venture was in direct competition with Belle's operations. When she heard of the affair, Belle broke it up. Holt fled the country and Eddie felt the sting of the quirt.

Word got to Judge Parker of Belle's son's capers, and his marshals were advised to keep a close watch on Eddie. The Judge was always anxious to strike at what he considered his most dangerous enemy, the Outlaw Queen. Then came the opportunity. In April, 1888, Eddie Reed was arrested for horse stealing.

Belle was furious. Now Judge Parker was tearing at her very heart. She realized Eddie was wild, yet she couldn't believe he would steal a horse. Why should he? She furnished him with the best horses in the country, and he didn't need money; she supplied that too.

Belle thought the charge against Eddie was false and trumped up, as her mind raced back to the same charges that had sent her and Sam to prison.

Belle jumped to Eddie's defense with all her resources—money, political influence and the press. In several statements in newspapers she said Eddie could not get a fair trial under Judge Parker because he was her son.

Whether Belle's statements were true or not, on July 20, 1888, Eddie Reed was found guilty of grand larceny and sentenced to seven years in the Columbus, Ohio Federal Prison.

Belle was shocked by the sentence. She couldn't bring herself to believe that even Judge Parker would hand out such a severe sentence to a seventeen-year-old boy, a first-offender. Again the press jumped on Judge Parker. The story got front-page coverage, calling the sentence revenge against Eddie's mother. The stories aroused the public, and much outspoken sentiment was expressed against Parker and his court. Several high-ranking government officials started calling for the Judge's removal from office.

The unusually harsh sentence was one of Judge Parker's biggest mistakes. To many it was obvious that the Judge, in his eagerness to strike out at Belle, had allowed logic to be overridden by a personal vendetta.

And once again Parker underestimated his adversary. Belle wasn't an ordinary person who would wilt and buckle and bury her head in defeat. Instead, she jumped on the defeat and turned it to an advantage. Many who before had scorned her as trash now took her side with sympathy.

Like a tigress aroused by an attack on her young, Belle took the fight to Judge Parker. She had her attorneys file an appeal, knowing it would accomplish nothing legally, yet it would serve to keep the story on the front pages of the newspapers. The press was responding with vicious attacks on Parker's inhuman form of "justice."

Just as in Blue Duck's case, Belle was laying a smokescreen to cover her real plan of action. Again she boarded a train for Washington, carrying newspaper clippings decrying Judge Parker and asking for his removal from office.

Belle's strategy and attack paid off. In a few weeks after her trip, Eddie received a full Presidential pardon. The victory over her enemy was a sweet one for Belle: not only had she gone over Parker and freed her son, but while in Washington she again stirred up the political pot. More and more powerful politicians started calling for Judge Parker's removal from office.

Judge Parker was furious—his image was tarnished and he was feeling the political pressure. His one-man rule over a vast domain was crumbling.

CHAPTER TWENTY-ONE

The short stay in prison didn't tame young Eddie. He returned to Younger Bend cockier than ever, believing his mother's influence made him untouchable. Wilder and bolder, soon after his release from prison Eddie was shot in the hip during a gunfight at Muskogee.

The wound was slight, but word reached Pearl in Missouri that her brother was near death, badly wounded. Pearl loved Eddie. Defying her mother's orders never to return home, Pearl left her baby with the Reeds and caught a train. She arrived in Eufaula, where she borrowed a horse from a friend and rode on to Younger Bend.

To Pearl's surprise Belle greeted her with open arms. And she was overwhelmed to find her brother none the worse for the wound.

Belle was happy to be united with her children again. To celebrate she took them to Hot Springs, Arkansas for a two-week vacation.

The Starrs returned from their vacation a happy, united family, having talked out their differences. Pearl seemed to have forgotten about her baby in Missouri and Eddie tamed down. Belle stuck close to her children.

Belle made big plans for her children. As a start she would clean out her outlaw lair and build a showplace home at Younger Bend. A big Southern-style mansion would replace the log cabin, and red barns and white corrals would hold blooded horses. Younger Bend would have social status. And Belle's children would have respectability.

To carry out her plans, in the fall of 1888, Belle retained an architect from St. Louis to come to Younger Bend and start drawing a set of plans for her dream.

Among other changes in her lifestyle, Belle started a reorganization of her criminal activities. She stopped dealing in stolen livestock and haboring criminals, and turned most of her attention to organizing vice in the region; it was more profitable and less risky.

The building of the railroads in the Choctaw Nation caused a boom in the coal industry. Belle had great influence with many of the Choctaw leaders, Green McCurtain, Benjamin Smallwood, Thompson McKinnly, Joe Folsom and others. She had worked closely with some of these men during the Cleveland campaign.

As the coal boom mushroomed and hundreds of coal camps sprang up in the Choctaw Nation, Belle took control of most of the vice, supplying entertainment of many varieties for the miners. Soon she had bawdyhouses and gambling halls running in many camps even though they were illegal.

The Choctaw Lighthorsemen had little interest in enforcing their laws in the coal camps unless some of their own people were molested. And Belle handed out favors to the U.S. marshals so they would turn their heads. There was one exception to these vices. Belle allowed no whisky to be sold in any of the places she controlled. The Choctaws were very strict prohibitionists.

Since no whisky could be sold in the coal camp a new alcoholic beverage, "Choc Beer" was created. Choc Beer, a malt brew, soon gained wide popularity with the miners. Belle soon had control of the new brewing industry.

Thousands of foreign miners were imported into the coal boom region. At best, working conditions in the mines were horrible. Conditions became so bad that the miners organized and struck. The mine owners (mostly Eastern) countered the strikes by bringing in strikebreakers, setting off much violence.

The foreign miners had few friends in the area. Everyone seemed against their cause—the U.S. Government, the Choctaw officials, and the mine owners. At the request of the mine owners Judge Parker sent a small army of his marshals into the strike-bound coal camps to keep law and order. But the lawmen sided with the mine owners and served more as strikebreakers than peacemakers.

Jim Greenhouse of St. Louis, a union organizer, met Belle and asked her assistance in helping the miners' cause, and offered her a large sum of money. Where money was involved Belle was always businesslike. So after some bargaining she accepted Greenhouse's offer. The money wasn't the only influencing factor. There was Judge Parker, his marshals and the railroads, all of whom Belle hated with a passion.

As always Belle laid out a plan of action. First she threatened several of the marshals with blackmail if they didn't lay off the strikers. Then she went to her friends in the press and retained J.W. Ownly, a prominent lawyer from Paris, Texas who had great influence with high-ranking Choctaw officials.

Ownly and Belle had several meetings with high-level Choctaw officials, convincing some of them of the miners' plight. The Choctaws agreed to meet with the union leaders and mine owner to discuss the labor problems. From these meetings better working conditions and pay scales were worked out.

Judge Parker learned of Belle's interference in the labor trouble and of her vice activities, and became furious. Belle was pleased at another insult to her avowed enemy.

CHAPTER TWENTY-TWO

During the mine strikes Belle met, and got, a new young marshal under her control.

One cold winter afternoon Belle was riding from Younger Bend to McAlester, following a back trail which led through dense wooded rough hills. Three to four inches of new snow covered the ground, making travel slow. At a fork in the trail she noticed a wagon had turned onto the road. The wagon was pulled by mules. Belle thought it strange that anyone would be traveling the rough back road with a wagon and team.

She studied the tracks as she rode. A short distance up the trail she saw another set of tracks enter the road. These were horse tracks. The two sets of tracks aroused her curiosity. She leaned in the saddle and studied the tracks more closely. From her years on the back trails she had learned to be an expert tracker and sign reader. The deeply cut wagon tracks in the snow told the vehicle was heavily loaded, and that the horse was carrying a rider.

Why would anyone be on the back road with a heavily loaded wagon? And why was a rider following? Belle rolled the questions around. Unless she was missing a guess, the rider didn't just happen on the trail by chance. He was following the wagon for a reason.

After another half-mile she was positive the rider was tailing the wagon and staying just far enough behind to stay out of sight. The signs showed the travelers were no more than a half hour in front. Spurring her horse to as fast a pace as was safe on the treacherous footing, Belle decided to get close enough to the travelers to see what was going on.

The trail made a wide switchback around a small mountain. Gaining rapidly on the travelers she decided to quit the trail and cut across the mountain. On the crest she pulled up to have a look. From the high vantage point she had a wide view. As she scanned the small valley below, the air was suddenly split by several shots.

Instinctively, Belle jumped from her saddle and jerked her Winchester from the saddle boot. Darting behind a big boulder she waited and listened. There were more shots, two different guns, a rifle and a shotgun.

The shots were coming from the west end of the mountain. Mounting up she picked her way through the rocks and brush. Then through an opening she saw a small ranch with a cabin, and a barn and corral off to one side.

A pair of mules were in the corral and a wagon parked nearby. Dismounting, Belle took her rifle and crept closer. As she studied the layout a rifle barrel poked around the corner of the barn. Then a voice shouted. "Wilson! You better come out with your hands up. I'm a U.S. marshal."

A voice roared from the cabin. "You go to hell. I've killed your horse. And I'll damned sure kill you." To back his words Wilson fired a blast from a window with the shotgun. Buckshot rattled the corner of the barn.

Belle moved down the slope toward the fight,

Winchester ready. She was curious about the marshal, and also, who he had cornered in the cabin. There was little chance of her being seen in the dense cedar brush. The two antagonists were too busy with each other to notice her approach. Circling, she worked closer to within about fifty yards, where she was well concealed, but with a good view of the situation.

The marshal ran to the other side of the barn, giving Belle a good look at his face. She had never seen him before. He looked like a kid not more than twenty years old. Too young to be a marshal, she thought, unless Judge Parker was robbing the cradle. She smiled.

Belle sized up the situation. The marshal's dead horse lay between the barn and the house. The setup looked like a Mexican standoff. If either man tried to leave his protection he would be a sitting duck. Leveling her rifle, Belle crept up behind the young marshal. The barn concealed her from the man in the house.

The marshal's full attention was on the house. Belle walked up behind him as he was shouting, "Wilson! Either come out, or I'll kill your mules."

That was enough. Belle stuck the rifle barrel to the young man's back. "Young sprout, drop your gun and turn around."

"Who? What?" the marshal mumbled in disbelief, feeling the gun in his back and hearing the woman's commanding voice.

"Lay that gun down and turn around real slow, kid."

The marshal hesitated, then stooped and laid his rifle on the ground. When he turned, his eyes widened. Belle said, "Kid, you claiming to be a marshal?"

His eyes nervously swept over Belle. "Yes ma'am, I'm a marshal. Name's Bob Hutchins, Judge Parker appointed me last week." He grinned and pulled back his coat. "See my badge?" Then the grin faded. "Are you that woman Belle Starr?"

"You guessed right, kid. Now take that six-shooter out of your belt and pitch it to one side."

Reality had soaked in. The marshal didn't argue, and tossed his gun to the ground. "How old are you, kid?" Belle asked.

"Eighteen, born 1871."

Belle smiled. "Damned if ole Parker isn't scraping the bottom of the barrel. Appointing school-boys is hard to believe. Anyway, now that we know each other, Mister Marshal, tell me - -what in the hell is going on?"

"First give me my guns back."

"Not until you tell me what this fracas is all about. Now talk up, or I might just trot you out there and let Wilson put the shotgun to you."

Hutchins studied Belle's eyes. Judge Parker was correct. She was a she-devil. He decided to talk. "See, this Wilson in there was working for old Ned Campbell over at Canadian. Old Cambell, he's about sixty and has got this eighteen-year-old wife. So this fellow Wilson ran off with Campbell's young wife."

Belle cut in. "So what? Happens every day. And young sprout, family problems are no concern of U.S. marshals. Hell I wouldn't blame Wilson if he did kill you . . ."

Hutchins interrupted. "You see, that's not all. Old man Campbell was in town when they left. They drove off with everything he had—wagon, team, furniture and two hundred cash."

"Still none of your damned business, stud."

"Let me explain. I ran into Campbell in Canadian, and he asked me to get back his wagon, team and money. He didn't give a damn about his wife."

Belle laughed. "You're learning the ropes fast. You're a sharp kid, and you know damned good and well this is none of your business." She eyed Hutchins. "Don't try to kid me. How much did Campbell offer you to get his things back?"

Hutchins lowered his eyes. "Fifty dollars, but believe me I'm no crook. I need the money."

"You need it bad enough to get blown into by a shotgun. You better take my word and get the hell out of here."

Hutchins stuck out his jaw. "I won't leave until Wilson pays for my horse he killed. I just rode up and hollered and the bastard shot my horse from under me. He is gonna pay me one way or the other."

"You're lucky he shot the horse instead of you, kid. But let me see if I can work this thing out between you and Wilson."

"Now can I have my guns?" Hutchins asked.

"I suppose so, but don't you start anything," Belle replied. Then she moved to the corner of the barn and shouted, "Wilson! Hear me. This is Belle Starr."

"Yes, I hear you. But you're not Belle Starr. She wouldn't have anything to do with the law."

"I'm not siding with the law, Wilson. Come out. I want to talk with you. You won't be harmed. I promise."

A long silence followed, then Wilson shouted, "Go to hell. I don't believe you're Belle Starr. I'm not coming out."

Belle turned to Hutchings. "Looks like were're going to have to force him out. I'm going to see this thing through."

Hutchins beamed. "You're gonna help me shoot it out with him?"

"Hell, no, don't you start getting any ideas. We're going to smoke him out." Belle paused and thought, then said, "While I keep Wilson busy, you circle through the brush to the back of the house."

"What for?" Hutchins asked.

"Shut up and listen. Climb up the wall and get on the roof. Then take off your coat and throw it over the chimney. The smoke will soon bring out Wilson and his woman. Remember now, no shooting. Now get moving."

Belle poked her rifle around the corner of the barn and fired a shot high into the wall of the cabin. Wilson blazed back with a blast from the shotgun. Belle threw a few more pot shots until Hutshins topped the roof and covered the chimney with his coat.

It didn't take long for the backed-up smoke to do the job. The door flew open and a man followed by a woman dashed outside, holding their hands over their faces, coughing and wheezing. Wilson managed a weak "Don't shoot. Don't shoot."

Belle approached the couple. "Calm down. You aren't about to be shot. Wilson, I said I wanted to talk to you, and I do."

In a few minutes the pair stopped coughing and rubbed the smoke and tears from their eyes. Belle said, "Listen, Wilson. I don't give a damn about you running off with this woman, nor about old man Campbell, but maybe you should pay the marshal for his horse you killed."

Hutchins jumped from the roof. "You're damned right, Wilson, you're going to pay for my horse."

"Shut up, lawman," Belle snapped.

Wilson brushed at his eyes and glared at Hutchins. "To hell with you. You had no call to follow us. This is none of your damned business. You're nothing but a sorry bast——."

Belle jumped between the two. "Cut out that damned jawing. Both of you are going to keep fooling around until someone gets killed." She backed off a couple of steps and leveled her rifle. "Now let's get on with the business at hand."

Wilson's woman broke in. "Honey, listen to her."

"Thank you, ma'am," Belle replied, then turned to Wilson. "You took two hundred dollars from Campbell. Now give the marshal half of it for his horse. That should be a fair deal."

"Hell, no, that nag wasn't worth twenty," Wilson snorted. Belle punched him in the gut with the rifle. "Look, I'm tired of messing around. Dig out the money and you keep the saddle and bridle."

Wilson rubbed at his red eyes and hesitated. His woman pleaded, "Give him the money, darling. Sounds fair to me."

Wilson dug into his pocket and pulled out a roll of bills. Counting out five twenties, he handed them to Belle.

"Now you two lovebirds go back in the house and start a nice honeymoon." Then she turned to Hutchins. "Come on, let's go."

The marshal followed Belle up the slope to where her horse was ground-anchored. She gave Hutchins fifty dollars. "Fifty-fifty split, my fee for handling the deal."

Hutchins took the money, wanted to argue, then changed his mind. Belle mounted her horse. "Jump up behind me. My horse will ride double. I'll take you to McAlester." She threw back her head and laughed. "And from what I could see of your dead horse, I don't think the critter would have ever made it. Wilson was right, it was real crowbait."

The day after the incident with the young marshal, Belle returned to Younger Bend to find Pearl and her girl friend frightened to tears.

When she inquired about the trouble, the girls related how the day before they had met a neighbor, Edgar "Bob" Watson, on a trail. He stopped them under the pretense of asking about a stray horse. Then he made advances. When the women refused he cursed and called them obscene names.

Belle knew Watson. He had moved into the region the year before, leased some land across the Canadian River, and grew a crop. The land adjoined a tract belonging to her. Always suspicious of strangers, she checked out Watson. He was wanted in Florida for murder and in Arkansas on a white slavery charge.

From the first, some of Watson's activities had confounded Belle. It wasn't unusual for a wanted man to settle in the Indian Territory. However, it was unusual for him to go around bragging he was wanted, as Watson was doing. The woods were full of U.S. marshals and bounty hunters.

Another thing about Watson which bothered Belle was his close friendship with Jim Middleton. Jim was the younger brother of John Middleton, the outlaw who eloped with Belle and was murdered. Belle had stayed on friendly terms with Jim after his brother's murder, but she didn't trust him. She thought he suspected her of leading John into the ambush.

Belle listened to Pearl's story about the incident with Watson. Then, without a word, she jumped on her horse and headed across the river toward Watson's home.

About a quarter mile from his house she spotted Watson with a wagonload of firewood. Riding with him was a youth. Watson was so busy talking that he didn't notice Belle's approach until she rode up alongside the wagon. "Pull up your team, Watson," she commanded.

Watson turned and reached for a shotgun lying atop the wood. Belle's hand flashed to her hip and a big forty-five was leveled. "Touch that gun and you're dead."

"What's wrong, Miss Starr?"

"Don't try to play innocent, Watson. Get off that wagon."

"But, Miss Starr."

"Shut your mouth, you son of a bitch, and slide off that wagon." A bullet smacked into a stick of wood, stinging Watson with splinters.

Watson jumped to the ground. "I haven't bothered you," he pleaded.

Belle swung from the saddle and punched Watson in the gut with the forty-five. "No, you haven't bothered me, but I'm sure as hell going to teach you to leave young ladies alone."

"What are you talking about?" Watson asked.

"You know damned well what I'm talking about, you son of a bitch—you insulted my daughter and her friend Mabel Harrison. And no one can do that and get away with it."

"They're lying."

"Shut up." She punched harder with the gun barrel. "Now get down on your knees."

Watson started shaking, sweat formed on his forehead. "Get on your knees, you sorry bastard." Belle's voice was like ice.

Watson dropped to his knees at the feet of the Outlaw Queen. "Please hear my side of the story Belle. I, ah—" His words were cut off. Belle jammed the gun barrel into his open mouth. Then, slowly and deliberately, she began working the hammer of the gun back and forth. For several seconds only the cocking and uncocking of the forty-five broke the silence.

Then she jerked the gun barrel from Watson's mouth with a quick upward yank so the gunsight ripped his mouth. A shower of blood sprayed Watson's face. Belle stood over the cowed man with the gun pointed at his head for several minutes. Then without another word she holstered her gun, mounted up and rode off.

Watson stayed on his knees for several minutes in a state of shock. After making sure Belle was gone the youth helped Watson on the wagon and drove him home.

CHAPTER TWENTY-THREE

The new year of 1889 came in with Belle at the peak of her power and with great future plans. Her children's futures were uppermost in her mind. She was planning to build the new home at Younger Bend and was working hard at trying to ingratiate their new stepfather, Jim July, to Eddie and Pearl.

The previous year July had been charged in Judge Parker's court with grand larceny. Belle planned to take July to Fort Smith on February 1, and answer the charge which her lawyer had advised they could get dismissed.

Belle and July planned to leave early in the morning, but were delayed a few hours. The night before Eddie had an all-night drinking binge. Not only had he stayed out, but he had taken Belle's prize stallion and ridden him into the ground. Belle was waiting with the quirt when Eddie came in at daylight. He was so drunk he fell off the horse. And while he was down Belle went to work with the whip. The quirt stung Eddie into sobriety and he fled into the brush.

It was mid-morning before Belle and July started their trip. Being late they rode hard. A little past noon they stopped near Keota at some friends of Belle's named McCann to rest their horses and eat lunch. When they arrived Belle found her friends in a state of sorrow. A small child had died just before they rode up.

The family asked Belle if she would ride to San Bois, several miles to the southwest, and take the news to some relatives. Always ready to help friends, Belle agreed and sent July on to Fort Smith, saying she would be there as soon as possible.

After finding the McCanns' relatives, Belle decided to spend the night in San Bois with some friends named White. Next morning she started to continue her trip to Fort Smith, but after traveling a short distance her horse became lame. Examining the horse, she thought it best to ride back to Younger Bend and change mounts.

It was a beautiful Sunday morning. Belle nursed her lame horse slowly along the trail, enjoying the early signs of spring which were raising their heads. Now and then she met a family in a wagon or buggy headed for church. Some she knew, and paused for a few minutes to exchange greetings. At Whitefield she stopped at Kraft's store, rested her sore-footed horse and talked with friends. After this brief stop she rode on to Hoyt, where she stopped at the home of Mr. and Mrs. Jack Rowe.

It was nearly noon, and the Rowes, being close friends, invited Belle to stay for lunch. Belle was helping Mrs. Rowe prepare the meal when, to everyone's surprise, Bob Watson and his wife Mandy drove up in a buggy. The Rowes, aware of Belle's run-in with Watson, were in an uncomfortable position. Not knowing what else to do, they invited the Watsons to eat, hoping they would refuse and leave.

To the Rowes' dismay, Watson accepted the invitation. Out of respect for the Rowes, Belle hid her animosities toward Watson and was very polite. But Watson, knowing he had Belle at a disadvantage, directed several slurring remarks her way during the meal. Belle didn't reply, hiding her anger.

After the meal the two men retired to the living room and the women began cleaning the kitchen. Watson left the living room and went back to the kitchen for a drink of water. As he passed near Belle he said, "Belle, your daughter is a liar."

Belle said nothing, calmly wiped her hands on a dish towel, then whipped a derringer from between her skirts. Mandy Watson jumped between Belle and Watson. Mrs. Rowe screamed, "No, no, my God, please don't, Belle!"

Jack Rowe ran into the kitchen and pushed Watson out the back door, then grabbed Mandy and shoved her after her husband. "Both of you stay away from my home," Rowe shouted.

Belle ran to the front of the house as Watson and his wife were climbing into their rig. "Watson, I'll see you later." Then she turned to the Rowes. "I'm very sorry, folks, I'll be going."

Mrs. Rowe said, "Belle, you don't have to go. You are welcome to stay as long as you wish."

"Thanks, Mrs. Rowe, I know that. But I must get home with my lame horse."

"No, don't go now, please stay awhile," Jack Rowe cut in.

To satisfy her friends Belle visited another hour. When she left, Mrs. Rowe insisted she take some cornbread muffins to Pearl. Even though they were good cooks, neither Belle nor Pearl ever mastered the art of baking good cornbread, of which both were very fond.

There were two routes from the Rowes' home

which led to a ford across the Canadian River to Younger Bend. One was an old wagon road which was once a section of the California Trail, the other a little-used trail circling around the Watson farm.

Belle took the road by Watson's house, even though the wagon road was the closer route. She rode slowly, letting her lame horse take its time. A quarter-mile east of Watson's place was a cross-roads separating the Watson farm from the Milo Hoyt land. At one corner of the crossroads was a dense patch of tall grass and weeds.

When Belle rode into the crossroads it happened — one of the most published pages of Western history was written. A shotgun blast roared from the weed patch. The charge of buckshot hit Belle in the back, knocking her from the saddle. She rolled on the ground, trying to dig her gun from its holster. The bushwhacker, seeing the Bandit Queen wasn't dead, ran from his ambush firing another shot point-blank. This blast ripped the fallen woman's shoulder and face.

Belle's horse bolted and sped home across the Canadian River. Pearl was standing outside the house when her mother's horse raced up, saddle empty. Pearl knew something was wrong. She caught the horse, a lump in her throat. Something was wrong. The saddle was covered with blood.

Her mother was hurt, hurt bad, maybe dying someplace back on the trail. Pearl jumped on the horse, then noticed it was lame. Jumping from the horse she dashed to the stables, caught and saddled another horse. Then she heard racing hoofbeats approaching. She didn't know what was going on, but she wasn't taking chances. Belle always kept a Winchester hidden in the barn for emergencies. Pearl grabbed the rifle and peeped through a crack in the barn wall. A rider slid his horse to a halt and shouted, "Pearl! Pearl!"

Pearl recognized the rider as Milo Hoyt, a close friend. "Down here, Milo. What's wrong?" she shouted.

"Pearl, it's your mother. She's hurt bad."

Pearl mounted the fresh horse. "Where? Where is she?"

"Across the river, up the trail. Follow me."

They raced down the slope and plunged across the Canadian River, both riders letting their horses have their heads over the rough trail.

About a hundred yards from the crossroads Pearl saw the crumpled form of her mother lying in the road. Spurring and lashing her horse to a greater effort she shouted, "Mother! Mother!"

Jumping from the racing horse, Pearl reached under her mother's head, raising and clutching it to her breast. "Mother, it's Pearl."

The black eyes opened. Pearl wiped at the blood streaming from her mother's torn face. "Mother, who did this?" Belle's lips quivered, but there was no sound. Then they closed forever.

Pearl didn't panic. She was the daughter of Cole Younger and Belle Starr. Gently she lowered her mother's head and covered it with the familiar white Stetson. Then she got to her feet. "Milo, go get your wagon and team and let's take Mother home."

Word of Belle Starr's murder spread quickly. Newspaper headlines blazed, "Belle Starr, Outlaw Queen, Murdered!" The nation was stunned.

Jim July was notified in Fort Smith of his wife's murder. He rode the eighty miles from Fort Smith to Younger Bend, changing horses three times along the way.

Milo Hoyt, Jack Rowe and Jim Newton hauled Belle's body across the Canadian River to her beloved Younger Bend home. Neighbor women gathered, bringing food and consoling Pearl. Cherokee and Choctaw women embalmed the body using wild native herbs.

A carpenter in Brairtown fashioned a simple casket. The body was dressed in a new black dress trimmed in white lace. Around her neck was placed a heavy jeweled necklace, and across her breast the long-barreled six-shooter given her by Cole Younger was lain, her hands across the gun.

The Starr clan took charge. Belle was one of them. They dug a grave about fifteen feet from the front porch of her home. The Bandit Queen was to be buried in the ground she loved.

One day after her forty-first birthday, Wednesday, February 6, 1889, Belle Starr was laid to rest. The service was held in the early afternoon under a warm sun. Hundreds gathered. Many were friends, others just curious. Also in the crowd were many news people and several U.S. marshals.

Members of the immediate family, Pearl, Eddie and the Starrs sat in the living room with the open casket. They were silent. Now and then one would walk to the casket, look and then return to his seat. Pearl's friend Mabel Harrison sat next to her.

There was no organized religious service. Several Cherokees and Choctaws said prayers in their native tongues. Mrs. Jack Rowe read some verses from the Bible. The crowd milled about outside and talked in whispers. Then at a signal six of the Starrs, acting as pallbearers, stoically carried the casket outside. All were armed. One of their clan had fallen to an unknown enemy, and revenge was on their minds.

The casket was placed on some saw-horses near the open grave. The waiting mulitude formed a ragged line and slowly passed by the open coffin. Some of the Cherokees dropped small pieces of corn-bread in the casket in keeping with belief of supplying a departed one with their favorite food for a long journey.

As the crowd passed, the Starrs and Jim July studied each face. They were looking for someone—the killer.

The sun was low in the blue February sky when the last mourner passed the casket. Yet, most of the crowd didn't leave. They bunched into small whispering groups and watched the casket lowered into the grave and covered with the soil Belle loved.

One of the crowd was Bob Watson. He brazenly walked by the open casket, to the amazement of many who knew of his trouble with Belle. Then he lingered while the grave was being filled. Jim July watched the last spade of dirt patted into place, then whirled with a Winchester leveled. "Put your hands up, Watson. You're under arrest."

Women screamed and the crowd scattered. They were sure July intended to kill Watson. Nervously, Watson looked about for help. Instead he met the deadly stares of the Starrs. His eyes turned toward three U.S. marshals standing nearby. They turned the other way. "You're not going to kill an unarmed man," Watson pleaded.

July moved closer. "You killed my wife."

Watson's voice was shaking. "Believe me, July, I didn't kill Belle. You have the wrong man." He looked at the retreating crowd. "Please don't leave. This man is going to kill me."

July snarled. "Watson, you coward, you're too

scared to even understand what I'm saying. I said you're under arrest. I'm taking you to Fort Smith. But if you resist I will kill you."

"Don't shoot. I'll go. But I want someone to go with me. You will kill me on the way."

July looked at Jack Rowe. "Mr. Rowe, will you go with me to take Watson to Fort Smith?"

Rowe nodded yes.

"Do you trust Rowe?" July asked.

"Yes," Watson replied.

After some conversation Rowe and a man named Jim Welsh agreed to make the trip. Eddie and Pearl went along as well. The group traveled all night, arriving in Fort Smith about noon the next day. July took Watson to the Federal Building and signed a murder warrant. It was strange none of the U.S. marshals at the funeral interfered or offered to accompany the group on the trip.

Watson denied the charge.

Watson was held in jail several months before he was given a preliminary hearing. There was a good reason for the delay—to let things cool off. Belle had countless friends and admirers, among them some of the country's toughest outlaws and gunfighters. She had provided many things to these men—leadership, security and to some their only contact with the outside world. Some of these badmen would have shot Watson on sight. Then there were some crackpots who would have killed him for the headlines. So the federal jail was the only place Watson was safe.

Finally Watson's hearing was held in late April, before United States Commissioner Brizzolara. The hearing was as strange as the other incidents surrounding Belle's murder.

The prosecutor presented a very weak case, not offering in evidence Watson's shotgun and two spent shells found at the murder scene.

Watson's only defense was his own testimony. He swore he was home and had nothing to do with the murder. His story was backed up by his wife. Also several people appeared as character witnesses, swearing Watson was a good honest man.

Belle's friends in the courtroom stated the character witnesses were strangers to them and didn't live in the Younger Bend region. Jim July, seeing he was losing his case against Watson, asked for a week's delay to produce more witnesses.

The request was granted. July rode to Hoyt to get the Rowes. He was certain their account of the run-in between Belle and Watson in the Rowe home before the murder would destroy Watson's defense. But the Rowes were both very sick with the flu.

July returned to Fort Smith and asked Brizzolara for another delay until the Rowes were well enough to travel. The Commissioner denied the request. July then rode back to Hoyt and got a written statement. However, the statement was not allowed as evidence. So for lack of evidence the charge against Watson was dismissed.

CHAPTER TWENTY-FOUR

In the few hours after Belle was ambushed, and as word spread, Younger Bend country was overrun with lawmen. Small armies of Cherokees, Choctaw Lighthorsemen, and U.S. marshals descended on the scene. Tracks and signs were studied, but little evidence was turned up. The swarms of lawmen and curious hangers-on tramping about worked to the bushwhacker's advantage.

Rumors quickly spread naming several suspects. The main ones were Edgar Watson, Belle's son Eddie Reed, and her husband Jim July.

After Watson's acquittal the rumors grew wilder. Watson began making open statements that Jim July had killed Belle.

Afraid to return to his home at Hoyt after his release, Watson stayed around Fort Smith stirring up suspicions about Jim July. But he was unable to convince the federal authorities of July's involvement. Apparently they were content to let the matter die.

But Watson did find one ear, Bob Hutchins, the young eighteen-year-old marshal. Being a schemer and fast talker, Watson had learned of Hutchins' fascination for Belle after they had met in the shootout near McAlester.

Hutchins was grief-stricken when he heard of

Belle's murder and in the right frame of mind for Watson to work on. The love-crazed young man took Watson's story as the truth.

Watson told the young marshal that July came to his home about an hour before Belle was ambushed and that July was drinking. After some talk July asked to borrow a shotgun, saying he wanted to shoot some wolves. Watson said he loaned July his shotgun, one barrel loaded with buckshot, the other with turkey shot. Watson went on to tell Hutchins that in an hour or so July returned the gun and that both barrels had been fired. Also he said he saw heel marks in the road which matched July's boots.

Watson also talked Hutchins into returning with him to Hoyt to get his personal belongings.

Returning to Fort Smith, Hutchins persuaded Marshal Heck Thomas to get a warrant issued for July charging him with bail jumping. Armed with the warrant, Hutchins went looking for July.

July, learning Hutchins was after him, disappeared. For almost a year the young marshal tracked July through the Indian Territory. July had many friends and was slippery.

But on the night of January 24, 1890, Hutchins caught up with July. Hutchins and Marshal Bud Trainor were drinking in a saloon in Ardmore and heard from a drunk that July was hiding in the vicinity. Asking more questions, the marshals learned July hid in a cave during the day and stayed with a friend, J.H. Salzer, at night.

The marshals learned Salzer lived a few miles north of Ardmore. The next night Hutchins and Trainor set up an ambush near Salzer's home. While they were waiting, Trainor, with a weakness for alcohol, got drunk. Just after dark July came riding along the trail. Hutchins opened fire without warning. July was critically wounded and his horse killed.

Hutchins loaded the wounded July on a horse and carried him to a hospital in Ardmore.

The confused young marshal gave many accounts of the shooting. He told authorities July opened fire first, then that he surrendered and tried to escape and was shot. He was convinced Jim July killed his wife, Belle Starr. Even as late as 1950, just before his death, Hutchins, in an interview with a *Denver Post* reporter, gave this statement: "It is my firm belief that Jim July killed his wedded wife Belle Starr, and I killed Jim July when he resisted arrest."

January 31, 1890, the *Fort Smith Elevator* carried this account of Jim July's death.

"Deputy Marshal Heck Thomas last Friday night returned several prisoners, including Jim July Starr who was wounded by Marshals Bud Trainor and Bob Hutchins. The trip was by train. This writer who was well acquainted with Starr visited him in the jail hospital Saturday and found him suffering from his wounds. He was asked if he was not running from the law when he was shot. He replied he did not run until after he was wounded and that they shot his horse three times killing the animal.

"Sunday we visited the jail again and found July in a dying condition. Thinking he might have a statement to make, the jailer informed him that the doctor had pronounced his case hopeless, and if he had anything to say he best do it at once. He asked to see his bondsman, Captain J.H. Mershon and said he would talk with

him, but no one else. He was told Mershon was
in Texas."

So Jim July died without making a statement
and was buried in a potter's field at Fort Smith.

July's friend Salzer tried every recourse at his
command to stop July's removal from the hospital
in Ardmore to Fort Smith. He reasoned with
authorities and was backed by a doctor, who said
July was in no condition to make the trip, and moving him would mean death.

That Jim July didn't murder his wife and was
himself killed in cold blood by a duped kid must be
accepted as a fact.

How the confused young marshal could have
believed Watson's story is difficult to understand
All Hutchins had to do was check. He would have
found that July was in Fort Smith, and he would
have had no way of knowing Belle had returned to
Younger Bend because of a lame horse. There were
many witnesses who would have verified July was
in Fort Smith, eighty miles away, at the exact
minute Belle Starr was shot.

CHAPTER TWENTY-FIVE

The rumor that Eddie Reed had murdered his mother was even more ridiculous than the charge made against Jim July.

The rumor was built around the flogging Belle gave Eddie for being drunk and riding her prize horse. After the whipping Eddie left home and went to stay with the John Blackwell family near Whitefield. With Eddie was Harrison "Kid" Draper, a runaway young man from Checotah. Draper had drifted into Younger Bend and, like so many other hard-luck youngsters, Belle allowed him to hang around. Being about the same age, Eddie and the kid became close friends. So when Eddie left home Draper went with him.

On the fatal Sunday Belle was ambushed, Eddie, Draper and another young man, Jon Crosby, went to Aunt Lucy Surrat's for dinner. After the noon meal the three spent all afternoon at the Surrat home.

Eddie didn't learn of his mother's death until the next morning, when Pearl sent Walter Neal to the Blackwell home to find her brother. The young man almost went into shock when told of his mother's death.

Even though Eddie Reed and his mother had several violent disagreements, he worshiped his mother with a deep admiring love. After being notified of his mother's ambush-murder, Eddie almost ran a horse to death getting to their home, and swore openly to track down her killer and kill him on the spot.

With Edgar Watson exonerated by a court, Jim July and Eddie Reed eliminated as suspects, then who did kill Belle Starr?

Regardless of the many theories advanced, research fails to pinpoint the murderer, but facts do raise some interesting questions and suspicions.

During her colorful and extraordinary life Belle Starr made many enemies, as well as countless friends. There is little doubt that some shed no tears over her death. Both her friends and enemies covered the range of the social scale. If an individual or group got in her way she stepped on them. She fought for her friends with the same zeal as she fought her enemies, no holds barred.

Belle's most bitter enemies were people in high places. And these people stood to gain more from her death than any other group

Issac C. "Hanging Judge" Parker was probably Belle's most bitter and avowed enemy. Through her political influence and maneuvering, the Bandit Queen had broken Parker's one-man rule. Parker made no secret of his passionate hatred for Belle. She had challanged and destroyed his kingdom.

Fanatical in his values and beliefs in male superiority, Parker felt disgraced that a mere woman had even dared stand up to his authority. The judge was also aware that Belle had infiltrated his court system and had access to most of his confidential information. He knew about her tactics: blackmail, bribes, and feminine charms to undermine and corrupt. This caused him to become suspicious of his court officers. He fretted and withdrew in his frustrations, while Belle watched with deep satisfaction and taunted at every opportunity.

Parker was aghast when Arkansas Congressman John S. Little referred to the judge's court as a "slaughterhouse."

However, Belle didn't have the satisfaction of celebrating her greatest triumph over Judge Parker. The very day of her funeral, February 6, 1889, a bill backed by Congressman Little and Senator George Vest of Missouri passed, allowing all of Parker's decisions to be appealed to the United States Supreme Court.

March 1, another act weakened Parker's power even more. This bill established a "White Man's Court" in the Indian Territory, at Muskogee.

Other than Judge Parker, Belle also made some powerful enemies when she became involved in the coal miner's labor problems. Some of the Eastern mine owners were disturbed about her activities. There were rumors her life was threatened.

Bob Hutchins told one story about an attempt to kill Belle. According to Hutchins, he and Belle were riding north out of McAlester along the Texas Trail when suddenly Belle jumped from her saddle, yelling, "Hit the dirt!"

Hutchins dived and rolled into a ditch beside Belle. She pointed to some big boulders along a ridge. A man was crouched in the rocks with a rifle. Hutchins shouted for the man to throw out his gun and come out with his hands up. Instead the man dashed into some brush and took off on a horse.

Belle and Hutchins gave chase and caught the would-be bushwhacker. After a little persuading the man gave his name as Johnny Painter from Arkansas and admitted he had been hired to kill

Belle. He claimed the man who hired him was named Woodard, Superintendent of the MK&T Railroad.

Hutchins and Belle took Painter to McAlester and confronted Woodard. Woodard claimed he had never seen Painter before. A heated argument followed, with Woodard sending an employee for the Choctaw Lighthorsemen. The Lighthorsemen ordered Painter from the Choctaw Nation.

Later on September 24, 1894, Painter was hanged in Fort Smith for murder.

After reviewing known facts, and in light of Belle's many battles with powerful enemies, some credence must be given to the theory that the Outlaw Queen was the victim of an assassination plot hatched by a conspiracy in Fort Smith.

Many old-timers claimed Judge Parker himself headed the conspiracy and that Marshal Heck Thomas and some other marshals were involved. If this theory is true, Edgar Watson was to be the trigger man in exchange for the dismissal of several charges against him. The charges against Watson were murder in Florida and white slavery in Arkansas. In support of the theory these charges were all dropped while Watson was in jail awaiting trial for the murder of Belle.

Watson's activities before the murder also raise some suspicions. Three years before Belle was killed, Watson fled Florida just one jump ahead of the law. He settled in Franklin County, Arkansas, where he was soon suspected of heading a horse-stealing ring. And he and his common-law wife Mandy were investigated by a federal grand jury on white slavery charges.

The Watsons were not indicted, but after being cleared they did some strange things. They didn't return to their home in Franklin County. Instead they stayed in Fort Smith two or three weeks. Watson spent most of his time hanging around Judge Parker's court. Being a smooth talker, he became friendly with several marshals. Then a strange series of events started.

Watson was without funds, yet he showed up at Hoyt looking quite prosperous. He had a wagon, team, farming tools, household goods, a large supply of livestock feed, groceries, and a lease on a Choctaw Nation farm.

His move into the Younger Bend Country, equipped to begin a farming operation, raises many suspicious questions. He wasn't a farmer; why did he suddenly take up the venture? And who would stake a man without any agricultural experience? But the most questionable part of the venture is how Watson secured the lease on the Choctaw-owned land. Tribal land laws were usually a three-party transaction involving the United States Department of the Interior, the Choctaw Nation, and the leasee. On his own it is highly doubtful that Watson had the right connections to obtain such a highly sought-after lease without help from influential people in high places.

According to old-timers Watson did little farming. Instead he spent most of his time riding about the countryside bragging about himself and flirting with all the women. He also did much gossiping about Belle Starr, even though he didn't know her. When warned his talk about the Bandit Queen was an open invitation to trouble, he laughed and said, "I can take care of the old Belle Cow."

Watson also seemed to have a list of certain people to contact in the region. Soon after moving into Younger Bend Country he paid Jim Middleton a visit at Brairtown. Jim, the younger brother of the murdered outlaw, John Middleton, lived on a farm with his mother. After John's murder Jim had openly stated that Belle had led the outlaw into the ambush.

Strangely, after meeting Watson, Jim tried to build a friendship with Belle. He began visiting her at home, causing Belle to wonder at his sudden change. She was polite to the young man, but suspicious and cautious.

When not roaming the area Watson made frequent trips to Fort Smith. He always used his real name, which was unusual for a man wanted for murder. Rumors circulated about the region that Watson was a detective.

If Watson was the trigger man, as the theory goes, then he almost blew apart the plot twice. First, his run-in with Belle over Pearl and second, the confrontation at the Rowes' home. Apparently he started both fracases, intending to shoot Belle in front of witnesses and claim self-defense. But the Outlaw Queen was too fast for him.

After the confrontation at the Rowe home Watson was scared. If he had been hired to kill Belle, then he had worked himself into a real jam. Through his own stupidity he had failed to do the job and would have to answer to someone. Belle would either kill him or have it done. Time had run out. He had to act fast.

A pure stroke of luck probably saved Watson and led to Belle's ambush. Shortly after he and his wife arrived home after being forced to leave the Rowe home, Jim Middleton rode up. He was accompanied by a horse trader named Hayes from Arkansas. Hayes had known Middleton and his family at Paris, Arkansas.

The horse trader was camped with a string of horses on Brooken Creek about three miles west of Watson's place. Somehow Middleton heard his friend was in the vicinity and rode over to the camp for a visit. During their conversation, Middleton mentioned Bob Watson. Hayes told the young man he had known Watson in Arkansas, that he was a tough character, and advised Middleton to stay clear of him.

They talked on and Middleton told Hayes that Watson was planning on selling his team and suggested Hayes might buy them cheap. Hayes said he didn't want any dealings with Watson. But after some more conversation he decided to have a look at the horses since he would be riding part of the way home with Middleton.

As the two rode toward Watson's place Middleton asked Hayes if he knew Belle Starr. Hayes answered yes, that he had sold her a horse once in Fort Smith.

When the two arrived at Watson's home he was on the front porch. According to Hayes, Watson was very nervous. Hayes asked Watson if he wanted to sell his team. Watson said he had changed his mind and didn't want to sell. So Hayes said goodbye to Jim Middleton and left.

What happened after Hayes left can only be a guess, backed up by some statements Middleton made many years later to some friends.

There was a conference. Watson told Middleton about his run-in with Belle at the Rowes'. Quickly a plan was devised. Watson could handle Middleton. He figured Belle would ride by his place on her way home.

After the conference, Watson gave Middleton his shotgun, instructing him to cross a field and hide in the weed-grown fence corner. Watson knew Belle would have to ride through the crossroads if she came by his place.

Watson explained he would take Middleton's horse and ride up the road, then wait for Belle at the crossroads. This would keep her attention averted while Middleton shot her in the back. The revenged-crazed young man followed Watson's instructions.

The speed with which the ambush was set up was apparent. One barrel of the shotgun was loaded with buckshot, the other with birdshot. It is inconceivable that even the most inexperienced bushwhacker would have gone after someone with one barrel loaded with light shot. Even the location of the ambush was a poor selection since the weeds offered scant cover, and no protection whatsoever for the bushwhacker in case the first shot missed.

Someone or something (probably Watson) had to keep Belle's attention, or she would have never ridden into such an amateurish ambush. Her twenty-five years of riding outlaw trails had honed her senses to such a fine edge, she would have spotted the trap immediately.

Her lame horse caused her to ride slowly after leaving the Rowes' home. She spotted Watson on Middleton's horse, and saw he had a gun on his hip. "This is great, the damned fool is actually going to try to shoot it out with me," she probably said to herself.

Few men would have had the guts to draw against Belle. Definitely not Watson. About twenty yards from Watson she reined up her horse. Having witnessed countless gunfights, the Outlaw Queen knew all the tricks. Pulling her horse's head high, she turned sideways in the saddle to make a smaller target. Her jet-black eyes narrowed and stared death. With her hand near the gun on her hip she shouted insults and a challenge at Watson. The answer was a blast from the shotgun in her back.

Jim Middleton had avenged his brother. He handed the gun to Watson, then took the back trails home. Watson stampeded Belle's horse, otherwise it would not have run. All her horses were trained not to panic from gunfire. Watson then ran across the field home. The ambush took only a matter of minutes, since Milo Hoyt, who lived only a quarter of a mile distance, heard the shots and came to investigate in a few minutes.

For many years no one suspected that Jim Middleton probably pulled the triggers on the shotgun that killed Belle Starr. Then rumors started, substantiated by facts, and added to these Troy Huneycutt, Jim Middleton's best friend, claimed Jim told him before he died that he killed Belle Starr.

Edwin P. Hicks, in his book *Belle Starr and Her Pearl*, draws the same conclusion that Jim Middleton killed Belle Starr.

Strange that none of the many other researchers who claimed to have solved the mystery of Belle's murder mentioned Middleton as a prime suspect. He was in the area and had a motive.

It could be that some of the writers knew about Middleton, but failed to mention him because he just didn't fit the script. Jim Middleton was a plain man, faceless. And to have the notorious, colorful Outlaw Queen gunned down by an ordinary dirt farmer would be a taunt to the wild and wooly West. Even Belle probably would have preferred a much more dramatic ending as the curtain dropped on her final act.

CHAPTER TWENTY-SIX

After her death, Belle's children gained almost as much notoriety as their mother.

Shortly after their mother's death Eddie and Pearl sold most of her holdings and divided the money. Pearl went to Rich Hill, Missouri to visit "Grandma" Reed.

True to his word, Eddie started searching for his mother's killer. Sure that Edgar Watson was involved, Reed began looking for him. After Watson left Hoyt he went to Fort Smith, stayed a few weeks, then vanished. Eddie traced rumors of Watson to Hot Springs, Texas and all over the Indian Territory·without even a trace.

Doggedly young Eddie stuck to his task of trailing Watson for two years. It was 1891 before Eddie got a serious lead. He heard Watson and a woman were living near Sallisaw under an assumed name. He rode to Sallisaw. There another strange incident occured. Near Vian, Reed was intercepted by U.S. marshals and arrested on a charge of bootlegging.

Eddie Reed wasn't in the whisky-running business; this fact was verified by many reliable people. He was dedicated to hunting down his mother's killer. The arrest raises more suspicious questions. Was Reed about to corner Watson at long last? And were some people in high places afraid Watson might talk if cornered, knowing he would probably squeal to save his own hide?

Eddie Reed was taken before Judge Parker. Probably Parker didn't even see the young man. Rather, there before him stood the image of his worst enemy, Belle Starr. The trial was a farce. Eddie Reed was found guilty. And again Parker threw the book at the son of the Outlaw Queen, seven years in federal prison.

This time the Hanging Judge was sure Eddie Reed would do his time. Belle Starr was dead and not around to go over his court and free her son. But Parker underestimated one other person, Pearl. She took up the battle with the judge where her mother had left off.

Pearl was in the courtroom when Parker sentenced her brother. She broke into loud sobs. Then suddenly her face hardened. The tears stopped. Slowly she stood and walked before Parker and glared at him for several seconds, then hurried from the courtroom. Later Pearl told a news reporter, "I saw him as the inhuman sadist devil my mother said he was, sitting there gloating at me and my brother, Belle Starr's children."

Belle Starr's baby Pearl was a baby no longer. She was a grown mature woman, a woman whose bloodlines bred a passionate loyalty to her kin which never backed off from a fight. But Pearl knew that to challenge and fight Judge Parker took more than guts and brains. It would take money. Lots of money, money she didn't have.

Along with many other traits Pearl, the daughter of Cole Younger and Belle Starr, had inherited her parents' intelligent, crafty, tough minds. Even though Belle had tried to keep her activities hidden from her daughter, Pearl was very observant. She knew the score. Men controlled the money and power. Pearl had watched her mother use her female wiles to move men around like checkers, studying each move carefully.

She would play the same game, using men to her advantage. Pearl did some thinking and laid her plans with detail and care. They would be much the same as Belle's, but with no violence.

With her future planned Pearl moved to Fort Smith. She no longer used the name Younger. She was Pearl Starr, daughter of the notorious Outlaw Queen. Using her mother's contacts with men in high places, Pearl soon established herself, and was ready to launch a career, a career that made Pearl Starr a legend almost matching that of her infamous mother.

In 1891, Pearl Starr entered the world's oldest profession: prostitution. Her plans were not to be just a common working prostitute, but to control the profession in Fort Smith.

Like her mother, Pearl researched and studied each move before it was made. To take over prostitution she knew she first must have experience and a thorough knowledge of bawdyhouse operations. To gain this needed experience she took up residence in a red-lantern house across the river from Fort Smith in Van Buren.

With her looks, intelligence and social graces Pearl outclassed the other girls in the house. She didn't lack for customers, but she chose them with care and for a purpose other than their fee. They had to have lots of money, or influence, preferably both. She let her customers know they were privileged to be having favors with a very special woman, "Belle Starr's daughter." Her fame spread quickly and was the talk of the border town.

In less than six months Pearl had the experience, financial backing and enough men in the right places to make her move. In 1891, at 25 Water Street, Fort Smith, Pearl Starr opened her own bawdyhouse.

"Pearl Starr's House" was located in the center of Fort Smith's red light district. At that date Fort Smith was a wild and wooly frontier town, the jumping-off place for the West, called "Hell of the Border" by some and "Judge Parker's Hellhole" by others.

In this sprawling, raunchy river town of 11,000 there were scores of saloons, all featuring gambling, dancing girls and other pleasures. And the town's red-light district, called the "Row," had gained nationwide notority.

Ideally located next to the railroads, river wharfs, wagonyards and campsites of the hundreds of travelers heading West, Pearl Starr's House flourished from the first day she opened the doors. And of course all the "young bucks" wanted to brag that they had met the daughter of Belle Starr.

It was in this type of environment that Belle Starr's "Baby Pearl" launched her business venture.

Using her mother's notoriety and her own cold calculating business methods, Pearl Starr gained a reputation which has never been equalled in another house of prostitution.

Pearl's approach to gaining her infamous popularity was just the reverse from the methods used by her mother. Belle grabbed the headlines with her wild flamboyant lifestyle, while Pearl played the part of the perfect lady—well-mannered, educated, dressed in the latest fashions with an innocent girlish look. Belle had tutored her baby to be a lady, and Pearl didn't go back on her training.

Pearl soon was recognized as the head madam of the Row. She recruited and selected her girls with care. They had to meet her standards and qualifications, not only of beauty, but intelligence as well. All of Pearl's girls had to read and write, be well-mannered and good conversationalists. She never used girls with emotional problems or ones who had been forced into prostitution by white slavers. All the girls at Pearl Starr's House entered the profession of their own choice, for money, adventure, or a husband.

Some of Pearl's employees married some of the most prominent men in the region. She usually had a long waiting list of prospective employees. It was known that Pearl's house had better working conditions and offered more opportunities and social status than any of the other houses on the Row.

Pearl entered prostitution on a mission—to make enough money and gain enough political influence to free her brother Eddie. In two years she had gained sufficient amounts of both to launch her battle, by following a well-thought-out plan: saving her money, making friends with influential men, and contributing to the right politicians' funds. With these resources Pearl used the same tactics as her mother—going over Judge Parker's head to the top, to the President of the United States, Harrison.

Colonel Ben T. Duval and W. M. Cravens of Fort Smith were retained by Pearl. Not only were they two of the best criminal lawyers, but they had political powers as well. After reviewing the case, the attorneys, accompanied by Pearl, went to Washington and gained an audience with the President.

The trip was a success. For the second time,

Judge Parker was forced to grant Eddie Reed a pardon.

Judge Parker was furious. First he had been insulted by Belle Starr, Queen of the Outlaws, now her daughter, Queen of the Whores, had belittled him.

CHAPTER TWENTY-SEVEN

Pearl met the train which brought Eddie from prison. After a tearful embrace they left the depot hand in hand to a waiting carriage. But before they drove away the two became involved in a heart-tearing disagreement.

Eddie was curious as to where and how Pearl had obtained the money to secure his release. At first Pearl claimed to have worked in a dress store and saved the money, but Eddie wouldn't believe the story. Then in tears Pearl had told her brother the truth.

Eddie was angered and hurt, his sister a whore and the madam of a house on the Row. He said he had rather lay out his sentence in hell. He told Pearl he was leaving and she would never see him or hear from him again. He also said, "Mother would turn over in her grave, Pearl, if she knew you had turned whore."

Pearl pleaded with her brother; he was all she had in the world since their mother was murdered. She had done it all for him.

Eddie loved his sister and gave in to her pleas on condition that she would forsake her life of shame. They would move far away, change their names and start a new life. But not until he had hunted down his mother's killer. She had to be avenged. He explained

243

he was as dedicated to this mission as Pearl had been to freeing him.

Pearl was against Eddie tracking down their mother's murderer. She argued it would only bring more trouble. But Eddie stood firm: their mother had to be avenged. After a long, heated argument, the two reached a compromise. Pearl would continue to run her business and supply Eddie with the money he needed to carry out his mission. Then they would to go South America, California or Mexico and start a new life.

With Pearl's financial backing Eddie again went on with the search for his mother's killer. He was out of prison only about a month when the most unbelievable incident in the unusual lives of Belle Starr's children occurred.

Eddie was at the old home in Younger Bend when a marshal rode in one day with a message that his presence was requested at a meeting in Fort Smith.

The meeting was in the offices of Pearl's attorneys Cravens and Duvall. There was nothing unusual about four of the participants at the meeting, but the fifth member in attendance was unbelievable: Judge Parker himself. What brought the judge to the meeting, and what was discussed, will probably always remain a mystery. However, an announcement made shortly after the meeting by Judge Parker shocked the country.

"Issac C. 'Hanging Judge' Parker Appoints Edwin Reed, a Deputy U.S. Marshal. Reed, Belle Starr's Son Is a Two-Time Convicted Felon in Parker's Court." When the news broke even

Parker's closest friends and associates shook their heads in disbelief. "What power did Pearl Starr hold over the old judge? Blackmail, or what?"

With the marshal's badge on his chest Eddie Reed rode to Claremore in the Cherokee Nation, with a tip that Edgar Watson was living near the community. This time the information proved correct, but someone tipped Watson and he fled before Reed arrived, leaving no trail.

Now 22, Eddie married his childhood sweetheart and settled on a small ranch near Wagner.

Records show Eddie Reed was a good lawman, fair and honest, a loner staying away from other marshals. In his spare time Reed tried to pick up the trail of Bob Watson. He was a young man in a hurry and on a mission. No clue was too vague, no trail too cold for Reed to check out in his search for Watson.

Time slipped by, but Eddie didn't give up his hunt. Money was no object; Pearl supplied that. One day in 1896, Reed and Marshal Heck Thomas were in McAlester looking for a Kansas train robber. As always Eddie began inquiring about Bob Watson. A storekeeper told him there was a rumor Watson had been seen recently in Dallas.

Again the rumor proved correct, but again someone had tipped Watson and he had fled. Eddie returned to McAlester and started asking questions, this time about Marshal Heck Thomas. Thomas heard of Reed's inquiries and the two had a heated exchange of words.

Disappointed, Reed returned to his home at Wagner and soon became involved in another strange incident. On Octorber, 24, 1896, two brothers, Zeke and Dick Crittenden, rode into town saying they were looking for Eddie Reed. The brothers were former marshals turned gunfighters and were close friends of Marshal Heck Thomas.

The Crittendens started drinking and raising a ruckus in town. Someone rode out to Reed's place and told him the gunfighters were raising hell in town.

Eddie saddled a horse, rode to town and tied up in front of a general store. Immediately the brothers began taunting him. However, Eddie kept cool. He knew their game and wasn't going to play. Someone had sent them to kill him. They were trying to badger him into drawing first, then catch him in a crossfire and make the murder appear self-defense.

Reed was too smart to be caught in a trap, having been trained by some of the best gunfighters of the Old West. For several hours the deadly game went on, the Crittendens riding up and down the main street taunting Reed. He sent for the town marshal to help him corral the two. But instead of coming to Eddie's assistance the town marshal disappeared.

By early afternoon, the gunmen, realizing Eddie wasn't going for their bait, started shooting up the town. A citizen, Joe Burns, was wounded. Reed had his back to the wall. He couldn't stand idle and watch innocent people shot and the town destroyed.

So, alone, the son of Belle Starr stepped into the street and challenged the two gunfighters. The Crittendens were drunk but deadly, their hands hovering above their guns. Eddie commanded they drop their guns and surrender.

The following gunfight was as spectacular as any ever fought in the Old West. A lone lawman facing two badmen in the middle of a hot dusty street, frightened townspeople peeping from windows, loud angry shouts—then blazing gun muzzles, whining bullets—grunts and groans as the hot lead smacked into human flesh. Then it was over. The Crittenden brothers lay dead. And Eddie Reed stood untouched, feet spread with a smoking six-shooter in each hand.

The Outlaw Queen had trained her son well. Dick and Zeke Crittenden were no match.

Reed was sure the Crittendens had been sent to kill him. And also sure it had something to do with his search for Bob Watson.

Soon after the gunfight two saloonkeepers in Claremore sent Reed word they had some information about Watson, and about the Crittendens gunning for him. Eddie rode to Claremore. Not suspecting any trouble, he left his guns on his saddle and walked inside the saloon. It was a trap. Two guns blazed in a crossfire and Eddie Reed dropped to the floor, dead.

So, like his mother Belle Starr and his father Jim Reed, Eddie Reed lived by the gun and died by the gun.

Ironically, Eddie Reed was killed the same month and year that Judge Issac C. Parker died, November 1896.

CHAPTER TWENTY-EIGHT

After the deaths of her brother and Judge Parker, Pearl gave up hope of ever finding her mother's killer. Yet her thoughts were the same as Eddie's, that Edgar Watson was involved and the ambush was the plot of a conspiracy.

With Eddie gone, Pearl devoted full time to running her business on the Row. There was nothing else. Soon she became Fort Smith's "Big Mama," rich and notorious. In front of her house hung a big red star, circled by a string of white pearls. The lighted sign became a symbol of bawdyhouses across the country.

Pearl made frequent trips to her old home at Younger Bend to visit friends and her mother's grave. She had a native sandstone tomb erected over the grave soon after Belle's burial. A few months later thieves broke open the tomb and stole the jewelry and gun from the body of the Outlaw Queen.

Pearl had the tomb resealed and a large marble marker placed at the head. Joseph Daily, a stone-cutter, was hired to cut the epitaph.

BELLE STARR

Born in Carthage Mo. Feb 5, 1848

249

Died Feb 3, 1889
Shed not for her the bitter tear
Nor give the heart to vain regret;
Tis' the casket that lies here,
The gem that filled it sparkles yet.

Even today Belle Starr's grave in Younger Bend is wild and lonesome, surrounded by a wilderness paradise, a fitting resting-place for the unusual woman who gained worldwide notoriety in a primitive world of men, the Indian Territory.

Was Belle Starr a "She-Devil," a "Revenge-Crazed Sadist," an "Angel," or was she a "True Pioneer" no better or worse than most other frontier people who settled the West?

Whatever the case, this small woman carved out an empire in a frontier wilderness where many strong men had failed.

The Author:

Stoney Hardcastle is a nationally known author, lecturer, and historian of early Oklahoma and Indian Territory. His publishing record includes more than one million words of fact and fiction, ranging from full-length novels to magazine articles.

He's the author of such well-known works as; *He Met The Devil, Real Medicine Men, Law of The Gun,* and *The Legend of Belle Starr.*

Stoney is a native of Oklahoma, free-lance writer, and is teaching creative writing at Eastern Oklahoma State College in Wilburton, Oklahoma where he shares his talent with aspiring writers.

BELLE STARR'S SECRET WINE RECIPE

While researching the Outlaw Queen's life, I interviewed an old friend, Lattie Ogden, several times. Growing up in the Indian Territory near Younger Bend, Belle Starr's headquarters, Ogden was a close friend with the Starr clan. Ogden was also one of Oklahoma's first State Legislators. Shortly after Belle was gunned down, February 5, 1889, some of the Starr clan gave Ogden her secret wine recipe. With no interest in wine making, Ogden tucked the recipe away in a box of old photos and other old papers where it stayed for many years until he gave it to me.

I wanted to publish the recipe in my first book, but the editors overruled me and I also filed it away. Recently, while cleaning out a file, I came across the recipe and decided to share it with others.

Yes, I did make a test run. Works Beautifully.

Stoney Hardcastle, Author

BELLE STARR'S WINE @

USE TEN GALLON CROCK

STEP ONE: 60 lbs. grapes, cherries, or blackberries

A.   Crush in another vessel and pour into crock
B.   Stir in 10 lbs. sugar
C.   Dissolve one package of dry yeast in cup of warm water, add by slowly stirring.
D.   Finish filling crock with warm water to within one inch of top, then cover with a cloth.
E.   Place crock in a warm place and leave for approximately one week, or until mash stops working.

STEP TWO:

A.   Remove mash from crock. Squeeze and press through a strainer. Throw away squeezed mash and pour juice back into the crock.
B.   Add 10 lbs. sugar, then fill crock with water to within four inches of the top.
C.   Cover crock with cloth and let stand one week, or until wine is clear and all foreign matter has settled to the bottom.
D.   Strain wine into bottles and seal. Gallon jugs work better than small bottles.

        Ageing is up to the individual.